Edmond Kelly

Evolution and Effort

And their Relation to Religion and Politics

Edmond Kelly

Evolution and Effort
And their Relation to Religion and Politics

ISBN/EAN: 9783337080396

Printed in Europe, USA, Canada, Australia, Japan

Cover: Foto ©Thomas Meinert / pixelio.de

More available books at **www.hansebooks.com**

EVOLUTION AND EFFORT

AND THEIR RELATION TO RELIGION AND POLITICS

BY

EDMOND KELLY, M. A., F. G. S.

NEW YORK
D. APPLETON AND COMPANY
1895

PREFACE.

SCHILLER's picture of Stupidity challenging the gods, "Hurl here your thunderbolts and see if my dark belly cannot hold them," represents only one attitude of human dulness; it furnishes no suggestion of that other condition, when, penetrated at last by the thunder of heaven, she appropriates and proceeds to dispense it on her own account. And yet this is the fate she prepares for every great idea; it encounters first the imperturbable inertia of prejudice, only in the end to become the weapon of that prejudice against the very enlightenment in the cause of which it originally started. The Gospel of Christ after centuries of contempt and martyrdom at last became the idol of its persecutors, and in their hands served to extort the recantation of Galileo. The gospel of Mahomet, which was directed against the tendency of Christianity to revert to polytheism under the guise of the Trinity, eventually became a sword in the effort of Arabia to conquer Europe; and so the gospel of Evolution, which rightly understood rescues the destiny of man from his environment in order to restore it to himself, has been made by mistaken interpretation to bolster the opposite doctrines of determinism and *laissez faire*.

For Evolution is playing a very different part in the development of the human race from that which it played in that of the lower animals. Before its processes were interfered with by human faculties of intelligence and choice, environment was everything; the animal and vegetable kingdoms were as completely subject to what was pernicious in it as to what served slowly to select and favour the individuals best fitted to survive; and though certain environments contributed to the survival of continually higher types, others permitted only of the survival of continually lower types; so that while one set of conditions produced man, others destroyed all life save that of sage brush in the desert or lichens in the arctic zone. The prevailing notion that evolution necessarily involves progress has often been shown to be a profound error; it is only under certain limited conditions that it tends towards advancement; under others it not only retards advancement but even results in degeneracy. Again, judging from a human standard, nothing can exceed the injustice of evolution, its cruelty, its wastefulness. Our attention has been directed too much to the survival of the fit, not enough to the sacrifice of the unfit; too much to the few that survive, not enough to the millions that perish. Fair though the face of Nature may seem when we consider only her bounty to man, she has been a cruel stepmother to these countless millions of her creatures which she has sacrificed to her favourite son. Nor should we fondly imagine that man will forever remain the chosen race. Far from it; the very fate that has befallen every other dominant species awaits also ourselves; it is a part of the scheme of Nature that we too should perish before a superior race or a less favourable environment. One thing alone may save us; one thing alone differentiates man in this struggle with Nature from other animals—the faculty of choice, the faculty by which we resist the very appetites through which Nature lifted us to the head of her predatory system, but upon which she counts for our ultimate decay.

The denial of this faculty of choice by a large part of the scientific as well as the religious world is believed to constitute a serious danger, for it tends to paralyse the effort through which alone man can successfully resist the forces in Nature which continually tend to drag him down. If we attempt to contrast the process of evolution in the world before the advent of man with the process since the advent of man, we shall be struck by the fact that in its first phase it encounters no conscious or intelligent opposition anywhere, whereas man is to-day opposing it strenuously at every step. Moreover, we shall also be struck with the fact that the more intelligent and strenuous the effort of opposition, the higher is the type of man produced. And so the rôle of human effort in evolution becomes the determining factor in human destiny.

If this be the case, it becomes a matter of importance to distinguish which forces of Nature are on our side and which on the side of the enemy, so that we may favour the one and resist the other.

Among the great forces in the world is religion. We tend to regard religion too little as a force, too much as an institution. And yet regarded as a force religion is probably the greatest ally man has; regarded as an institution she has been sometimes in the past, and doubtless is still to a less extent to-day, his greatest enemy.

This book is an attempt to rescue the force from the institution; to establish its place in the new process of evolution in man as contrasted with the old process which preceded man; to determine its relation to science, to wisdom, to human effort; what are the limits of effort; how they are determined by environment, how far they depend upon conscious choice; the lines along which effort should be directed; the great problems of the world such as pauperism, socialism, education; through what agency they can best be solved; the rôle of the State; the neglected and yet indispensable instrumentality of politics—and this with a view to presenting an argument in favour of an alliance between politics and religion in the struggle of man with evil and with pain.

This book was practically completed before the reanimating results of the New York city elections in 1893. It would be a mistake to suppose that these elections have in any way disposed of an or-

ganisation which still finds 109,000 supporters out
of a total vote of 263,000. The elections, however,
do show that the people of this country can still be
depended upon, and that if the good elements in it
will, instead of dissipating themselves along gratu-
itous lines of individual action, co-operate along the
imperative lines of collective action, popular government can still be practically, as well as ideally, vindi-
cated. But to achieve this we must learn the lesson
that the State, to which we have confided the solution of our problems, is the instrumentality through
which these problems may best be solved, and that
the State can be rendered fit for this gigantic task
through the practice of the gospel of effort and
not through that of *laissez faire*.

CONTENTS.

EVOLUTION AND EFFORT.

16691

CHAPTER I.

THE CONFLICT OF SCIENCE AND RELIGION.

WHEN in the lusty vigour of our youth we first discover the logical defects of our creed, it is with a triumphant sense of escape from bondage that we enrol ourselves among freethinkers. This plunge into unbelief is a necessary phase through which most young men pass who at all struggle to free themselves from parental and educational control. It is a leap from the shelter of the nest into the freedom of the air, the discovery of strong pinions and the joy of self-reliance. We little know then over what a dark, tempestuous, and unknown sea we have stretched our wing. But when, after calamity has darkened our lives, some ritual of baptism or marriage or death brings us once more within the walls of the church we had in younger days with so light a heart abandoned, our memories are moved by old associations recalling, perhaps, a vanished hand or a silenced voice; the words of Scripture which familiarity had once sterilised for us become alive with new meaning; the music through

1

which it had once been a weariness to have to stand
brings an indistinct but no less consoling message
to our ear; and there comes to us through all these
channels the enquiry whether indeed this Christian
dispensation is in truth as much to be ignored as we
once in the pride of our youth imagined.

Unfortunately, the occasions on which such enquiries are started in our minds are few, and the
forces engaged in stifling them many. Amongst
these last there is none, perhaps, so potent as the so-
called conflict believed to exist between science and
religion—the conflict which once drove us from the
Church, and which must, so long as it lasts, keep us
exiles from its cathedrals, its ceremonials, and its
consolation.

Important, then, above all other questions to one
who has lived the arid life of an agnostic, is the enquiry just what this conflict between science and
religion is; what are its limits and what is to be its
final outcome. For, however rational the attitude of
the agnostic may be, there come moments when a
pang at the heart tells him that " man cannot live
by bread alone," and he asks himself whether he is
always to be driven without rudder or compass over
a black and coastless sea and never cast his anchor a
single day.

What, then, is religion, what science, that they
have joined issue with one another to the destruction of so much that seems useful and precious in
the world?

Science is easily defined : it is knowledge of the laws of Nature. Nothing can be more simple, nothing more necessary, than such knowledge as this. Even the orthodox will admit that we owe it to God as well as to ourselves to study and know his laws. But before man knew much about natural laws he was deeply concerned with what, for want of a better name, we may call supernatural laws. At another time it will be interesting and indispensable to trace with brevity, though with care, the development of this instinct which sets us upon an enquiry as to how we came into the world, why we are here, who made us, and to what end ; but, above all, as to the problem of pain, its justification, and how to escape it, if at all. But at this time let us content ourselves with noting that out of these questionings there sprang up among men various hypotheses regarding the Creator, the immortality of the soul, the hereafter, which became inseparably connected in the mind with ethics or conduct because they were all concerned with the same thing—the higher nature of man.

These rules of conduct were gradually developed by the necessities of social life ; but they were necessarily associated with the religious instinct, because both religion and social life call upon man for the exercise of the same faculty, viz., self-restraint. Religion, then, gradually covered two very distinct domains—that of metaphysics or theology, and that of conduct or ethics. It is the domain of conduct which concerns us first.

There are two ways in which man seems to have arrived at rules of conduct : By the assumption of a God, omnipotent, omniscient, and relentless; issuing his commandments to the world, promising reward to those who obey, and vowing punishment to those who violate them. This barbaric notion of a heavenly despot has, as civilisation advanced, become tempered by mercy; love has in a measure cast out fear, and, whether through the teaching of a Buddha or the life of a Christ, the heavenly message has become attuned to a less remorseless generation. This method builds its foundations in heaven and lets down, as it were, a ladder to man up which he may climb to spiritual habitations. Such is the religious method, or the method of revelation.

A second method is in its procedure directly the inverse of the first. In it there is no assumption, no mandate, no revelation. Man is studied as he is and as he has been, not through any flight of imagination, but through a cold, emotionless study of fact. Every source of knowledge is ransacked for contribution to the great central enquiry; astronomy fixes the place of the world in cosmos; geology, chemistry, and physics determine the conditions under which life made its way into the world, and biology tells us the method of its development, the story of each and all being weaved and interweaved so as to re-enforce and illustrate one another. If, as is claimed, this investigation tells in broken, perhaps, but no less certain terms the history of man's development from an amorphous and practically vegetable cell; if in the course of this development there is found to be an evolution of conduct as well as of function, so that as animal life becomes more and more intelligent it becomes more and more capable of conduct; if in this so-called evolution of conduct there is traced a development of sympathy, keeping pace with the development of function, so that the lowest forms of animals are found to be the most selfish and the highest forms least so; if the scheme of Nature is found to be such that in proportion as wisdom and love prevail, happiness prevails; and if, in short, the result of this investigation is to preach to men a gospel indistinguishable from that of Christ, what becomes of this so-called conflict between science and religion? For the method last described is the scientific method, or the method of research.

And so we have here these two so-called irreconcilable enemies—the religious method, or method of revelation, building its foundations in heaven and reaching down from heaven to man, and the scientific method, or method of research, building its foundations on earth and reaching up from earth towards heaven—both meeting in the same conclusion, both preaching the same gospel, both laying down the same rules of conduct. Is this a conflict, or is it a reconciliation?

That religion and science should have seemed to conflict with one another was inevitable; they start from diametrically opposite points, and deal with diametrically opposite temperaments. The religious are forever looking upwards, away from the concerns of the flesh and towards the aspirations of the spirit; they disregard the body, and would fain nourish only the soul; and by a natural exaggeration so despise their material needs that they tend by neglecting them to break down the very machine upon which the soul depends for its transfiguration in this world. The fact that the spiritual man seems to prosper only at the expense of the material man naturally sets the hopes of humanity outside of this world beyond the grave, and thus this world becomes a mere place of trial for an ultimate though unknown destiny.

Men of science, on the contrary, are agnostic of things divine, but not for that reason necessarily any less conscientious in their effort to understand the human mission. They begin with a study of the facts that surround humanity, carefully distinguishing these facts from the magnificent and comfortable assumptions upon which religions are built; and, strange to say, man, instead of losing in dignity from this point of view, becomes enhanced beyond the expectation of those who first had the temerity to adopt it. He ceases to be the creature and slave of an unknown God in order to take his legitimate place as the head and front of all created things—the ultimate result of an evolution that has been ceaselessly at work through immeasurable ages; no longer an unconscious nor helpless factor in another's game, but fully aware of his own powers to advance or hinder his fate, the architect of his own fortunes, working out his own salvation in this world which is his, with powers that are his, both of which are within his comprehension and in great part within his control.

Nothing could be more opposite—nay, contradictory—than these two theories of man; and yet nothing could be more identical than the rules of conduct which they respectively impose.

Science points out that ethical evolution has kept pace with animal evolution, though the former is traceable only at a later period. There is no room for ethics where there is no consciousness, and there is no evidence of consciousness in the lowest forms of animal life. Nor is there much room for ethics until animal movements seem to respond in some sense to intention. As soon, however, as intentional movements can be traced, it is observed that physical development is attended with a development of what for the absence of a better name must be called love. The animal ceases to be a solitary individual automatically engaged in maintaining his own existence, but begins to regulate his movements in sympathetic relation to others of his own species. At first this is confined to momentary and purely physical contact between the sexes; then the contact becomes extended to cohabitation; next there ensues care of the young by the mother; next, care of the young by the father; next comes herding irrespective of sex or parentage, so that the love which began by being purely sexual becomes in the second stage parental, and in a third stage tribal.

2

The more extended the sympathy the more ethical is
the relation. Thus we find parents sacrificing themselves more and more for their offspring, and individuals labouring not only for themselves, but for
their group; the wild goose playing sentry for his
flock, the bee gathering honey for his hive, the
ant collecting sticks for his hill. And so in animal
life we find the embryo of those affections which in
man ultimately develop into love which is conjugal,
parental, and tribal. When extended beyond the
tribe to the nation, this love clothes itself in the
garb of patriotism, and, last and greatest of all, results in the kinship of man to man, which outgrows
patriotism and extends its scope to men of all nations and of every clime. In this last development
love breaks the bonds of selfishness that make domestic and patriotic devotion only a form of self-
consideration, and conceives of man as having a
mission on earth rather than in heaven—a mission
dictated by no self-asserting authority, but imposed
by natural laws through which we move and have
our being; a mission that is written in the book of
life rather than in the book of so-called inspiration,
and one that demands as high a standard as any religious creed.

Doubtless it will be urged by champions in both
camps, who, disposed by temperament for battle,
will not hear of reconciliation, that the preceding
picture is not a faithful portrait either of science or
of religion; that it is conceived without regard for
fact to bolster a transparent compromise; that, in

fact, the description is constructed for the event, and not the event mirrored by the description. It is confidently believed that this contention is due to the fact that whereas most of us are agreed as regards what science is and what science teaches, we are profoundly disagreed as to what religion is and what religion teaches.

No attempt to describe the process of teaching conduct adopted by any particular church or religious institution would in this connection be practicable. In its detail, then, the description cannot fit any existing church or religion, but in its essence it must be common to all; for the religion or church that ultimately survives in any given time or place must be the one that most effectually in that time and place teaches charity, because charity is the necessary antidote to the selfishness upon which our civilisation is constructed, and no civilisation constructed upon this poisonous basis could survive unless the antidote were growing by its side. The fact which political economy has pointed out—and for pointing out which it has been roundly cursed by those who were unable to comprehend more than one half of the social problem at a time—is that our whole system of commerce is built upon the principle of human selfishness; and not a merely passive selfishness, but selfishness in the aggressive form known as competition. This is not a theory of political economy; it is a fact to which none but dullards and visionaries can close their eyes. Strange to say, the palpable terrible fact that men and women

out of church are at perpetual war with one another
helps to keep alive the institution under whose be-
nignant wing and in whose holy places once a week
at least our fellow-beings may meet under conditions
compatible with loving-kindness. Six days for fight
and one for love may seem an unequal distribution;
but, on the other hand, it must be remembered that,
such is the demand of the warlike in man for peace
and of the peaceful in man for war, the six days of
battle have been largely tempered by brotherly love
and the one day for peace cruelly sacrificed to the
ecclesiastical drum. Be this as it may, while the
battle for existence has taught men to fight one
another, the gospel of Christ has been telling them
to offer the unsmitten cheek; so that with the
week-day dose of malarial poison and the Sunday
dose of quinine, man must be admitted to have
had a pestilential time of it. So much, then, only is
claimed for religion, that, encrusted as it may have
been with *aberglaube* and bafflingly concealed by
superstition, the lesson it has laboured ineffectually
but perseveringly to teach has been the lesson of
charity and loving-kindness. Whenever it has
taught the reverse it has itself staggered under the
consequences, so that, out of its swings between the
fleshly lust of a Borgia and the spiritual lust of a
Torquemada on the one hand, and the transcenden-
tal mission of superhuman unselfishness on the other,
the final and surviving result of Christian teaching
has been the same as in the earliest dawn was an-
themed to the shepherds in Palestine: " Glory to

God in the highest; and on earth peace, good-will towards men."

But every religion ultimately suffers the fate of every great idea; it builds up an organised propaganda which becomes more powerful than itself. The propaganda continues to increase, but the idea it was organised to propagate takes a secondary place. More than this, the religious institution gradually finds itself in conflict with the very idea it was organised to propagate; for the religious idea once accepted becomes so simple, so eloquent, so unanswerable, that the vast machinery which at first the dulness of humanity rendered necessary, and afterwards the rapacity of humanity found convenient, is finally discovered to have become a bewildering encumbrance. The plain rules of morality taught by Christ become encrusted with theological discussions and unessential details; the simple devotion of the fishermen of Galilee forgotten in the pomp of a papal court.

In a similar way the Republican party in the United States, organised to suppress slavery and preserve the Union, when it had accomplished both, ought logically to have disappeared; but the vast wealth and potentiality of wealth which every great organisation affords to the skilful few who control and the many who profit by it were too tempting to be abandoned. Moreover, the vast machinery of a national party, however antiquated its principles, can serve an honest as well as a dishonest purpose—it can push a new issue, it can foil a new error, it can serve to check the arrogance of a rival national party. So, what with the new questions which perpetually harass the public mind, the tendency of the opposing party to go wrong, and the large personal interests involved, the Republican party keeps itself alive through appeals that are often insincere to so-called "party loyalty," assisted by large contributions to the protection fund.

So also Christian creeds, pursuing the great work of their founder Christ, have created establishments, built churches, universities, asylums, hospitals. They have served the purposes of bad men and fulfilled the aspirations of saints: they have distributed in charity and licentiousness the mite of the widow and the surfeit of the millionaire; and they have so wound themselves about the hearths and memories of our youth that outside of them there seems to be nothing sacred, and in them only can we hope to found a home on conditions of durability, happiness, and self-respect. Our minds may rebel against the baseless assumptions of Christian creeds, but our hearts will continue to lean fondly on the sentiments that cluster around the church organ and the Gothic arch.

The Christian system, therefore, survives the decay of its creed and will long survive it, because it continues to do good, to sustain the weak and to cheer the strong; because religion is an essential and not an accidental factor in the structure of man, and because it occupies a place which must remain occupied, and for which we have not as yet found any substitute.

And so religious institutions tend to become providential evils — evils because they perpetuate abuses under the name of religion, and providential because they perpetuate religion in spite of these abuses.

For positivism and agnosticism are no substitutes for Christianity : one offends because it is too positive, and the other because it is not positive enough. Neither appeals to any part of us except the reason, and no religion has ever survived that was founded on reason alone. For although we may intellectually assent to the propositions laid down by science, emotionally we cling to the ritual hallowed by memories of childhood, to music we have grown through long familiarity to love, and to the baptismal font and the altar step, which somehow we associate with pure women and as yet untainted youth.

Whether this compromise will last long is a speculation into which it is not necessary to enter; the practical question for us is how we can best conform our conduct to it, and how far give to it the apparent sanction of outward observance.

As a matter of fact, the true character of the compromise is revealed chiefly in the matter of ceremonial observance : women and children go to church, men stay at home; women observe Sunday, men do not; women pray, men work. It is not easy for a man who has been over-worked during the week to devote one day of rest in seven to ceremonial forms

which mean nothing to him. Occasionally, when a
child is to be baptised, confirmed, or married, a
ritual that at other times has seemed sterile becomes
clothed with significance, and reveals how much of
the old religion clings to the ruined temple in him;
then, perhaps, he thanks God that he has never altogether abandoned the shelter of the church. But a
tired body and a rebellious mind will in the end re-
gain their sway, half-formed resolutions to resume
religious observances will be forgotten, and Sunday
will become once again a day of well-earned rest and
relaxation. In very truth it cannot well be otherwise. The church service is not in itself a sufficient
reason to compel an attendance which, in the absence
of special stimulus, becomes unprofitable and intol-
erably burdensome; and so educated men, all the
more potentially useful to the community because
they are educated, doing their duty in their respective callings, are kept out of touch with that most
puissant of all the forces that have ever moved man
—religion.

This seems all the more intolerable and unnecessary, because, as has been already pointed out, the
gradual extension of sympathy or love which science
shows to have accompanied the physical evolution
of man in the past, and to give the best promise of
physical evolution in the future, is no other thing
than the doctrine of discipline and forbearance
which every religion that deserves the name has
taught since the world began. Is it conceivable
that no neutral territory can be found upon which

men of science and men of religion can join
hands?

The fact is, that if every self-styled scientific
man were truly scientific, and every self-styled religious man were truly religious, there would never
have been any conflict between science and religion.
The conflict is not, and never has been, between
science and religion, but between science-loving men
who disparage the Gospel and Gospel-loving men
who disparage science; combativeness falsely inter-
preting the Gospel on both sides is the real culprit.

Science appeals to the mind; religion appeals to
the heart. Some men have much head and little
heart; let them, if they will, be votaries of science.
But most men have more heart than head; offer
them science, and to the hungry you are giving a
stone. Logic indicates, and experience has proved,
that with these men religion is a mighty power—
for evil if in the service of evil, for good if in the
service of good. Well-balanced men have both
head and heart; such as these need religion no less
than science; and science itself teaches that perfect
development lies along the line of emotional as well
as intellectual progress. But not only do science
and religion appeal to different types of men, and to
the same types in different proportions, but they
deal with different subjects, or if they deal with the
same subjects, do so in a different way. Two examples will serve to illustrate this contention.

The conflict of capital and labour is one of the

most dangerous conflicts which are at present divid-
ing us. What advice has religion to offer? what
solution, what rule of conduct? Read, if you will,
the encyclical of the Pope on this subject, or the
exhortation from Protestant pulpits. Condensed,
they are all reducible to this : " Capitalists, be more
generous ; labourers, be less exacting." And yet
the labourer can hardly be characterised as exacting
who asks for no more than certainty of work, starvation wages while at work, and support when
superannuated ; nor can the capitalist be characterised as ungenerous who can truthfully answer that
competition prevents his guaranteeing any of these
three.

While, however, religion has little useful to suggest as a remedy for this tremendous evil, economic
science, collecting the results of experiment in England and France, offers an undoubted though perhaps incomplete solution :

In England, co-operation has successfully replaced competition in the distribution of necessaries,
but has failed successfully to replace competition in
production ; in other words, the co-operative stores
where things are sold on the co-operative plan, as
at Rochdale and the Army and Navy and Civil
Service Stores, have proved prosperous and advantageous, although efforts to introduce the system
of profit sharing in manufactories, under which the
labourer becomes practically a partner in respect of
profits, have failed. Had we, then, only the experience of England to go by we should have to record

a very incomplete solution. But at this point comes the experience of France, where a diametrically opposite state of facts presents itself. Co-operative stores have in France signally failed, whereas profit sharing has been attended by encouraging results, not only in the diminution of strikes but in the elevating of the workmen and in the process of suppressing the conflict between capital and labour, by making the capitalist and the labourer one. And so the science of political economy, ever engaged in collecting facts, sorting them, and deducing principles from them, is at work in England at determining the rules which have made there co-operation in distribution a success, and the mistakes which have made there co-operation in production a failure; and conversely in France the same science is arriving at a set of principles by which co-operation in production may be transplanted to England and acclimated there. Here, then, where religion stood powerless and baffled, economic science steps in with a solution.

On the other hand, the exact opposite may seem to be true if we glance for a moment at the political condition of our great cities in the United States. Those versed in the science of municipal legislation have vainly striven, by the application of this science to the municipal problem, to arrive at a solution; laws have been changed over and over again in the vain quest; every conceivable scheme of automatic government has been propounded, discussed, and sometimes applied; the ineradicable

unwillingness to recognise the real source of the
trouble has predisposed the minds of our citizens to
believe that the difficulty resides in our laws and
not in ourselves, and we have therefore patiently
stood by to see experiment after experiment tried,
although in our own experience we ought to have
found sufficient reason to be satisfied that nine
tenths of these experiments must end in discouraging failure. No better illustration could be given
of this than the changes that have taken place in
the laws of the State of New York on the subject of
the mayor's power of appointment. Prior to 1870
the appointments to office made by the mayor were
subject to confirmation by the board of aldermen.
Tweed, who was then at the head of the historic
"Tammany Ring," desiring to concentrate power
in the hands of the mayor, and thus escape the necessity of trafficking for every appointment with the
board of aldermen, changed this provision of the
law in the so-called Tweed charter of 1870, which
provided that thenceforth the power of appointment
by the mayor should not be subject to confirmation
by the aldermen. When the Tammany Ring was
overthrown in 1871 by the Committee of Seventy,
this committee very naturally restored to the aldermen the power of confirmation which had been
withdrawn from them by Tweed. In doing this
they pursued the system of checks and balances so
dear to American institutions. It so happened that
for some years after 1871 New York elected good
mayors and bad aldermen. The result of this was

that the mayor could not get good appointments confirmed by the aldermen, and had generally to capitulate to the aldermen by either withdrawing a good appointment and making a bad, or by some other concession of an equally demoralising character.   Moreover, it became impossible to know which of the two—the mayor or the aldermen—was responsible for the bad appointments, because a mayor could always throw the responsibility for such appointments upon the board.   The reformers therefore, in 1884, led by Theodore Roosevelt, demanded and secured the passage of an act that relieved the mayor from the necessity of going to the board of aldermen for a confirmation of his appointments, thereby, strange to say, restoring the distribution of political power to what it had been under Tweed's dishonest rule.   The result of this last law was exactly what a very little political sagacity might have foreseen.   The evil element in the political community, which before 1884 had contented itself with electing bad aldermen, now devoted itself to electing a bad mayor, and since the enacting of this so-called reform law of 1884 the mayor's chair in New York has been filled until to-day by an unbroken succession of Tammany candidates.   The real evil lay beyond the reach of political science or legislative enactment; it lay in the indifference and discouragement of all those citizens who were not engaged in politics for private or for partisan purposes.   This indifference was a question not of political science but of private conduct; it could be reached only by such influences as are generally termed religious, because they appeal to man's ethical sense against the evil tendencies which surround him. This whole incident furnishes an admirable illustration of the truth of Montesquieu's contention, that the welfare of a republic depends upon the virtue of its citizens. When citizens have ceased to be virtuous, or when virtuous citizens have abdicated in favour of admittedly corrupt political machines, it is hopeless to expect that the government can be made good by changing the distribution of political power amongst the thieves to whom it has been abandoned. Nothing, therefore, but an awakened sense of the duties of citizenship can reach the evils of municipal misgovernment. Where shall we find the voice to awaken it?

Now, although science may justify to us the Christian rule of "enlightened altruism," it has as yet utterly failed in inducing men to make the sacrifices necessary in order to conform to it. A few men of cultivated brain and philosophic temperament do undoubtedly, with a positivist ritual or without any ritual under the agnostic flag, lead lives of righteousness and morality; but neither positivism, nor agnosticism, nor any purely intellectual ism has as yet kindled enthusiasm among the masses, or reached the masses at all; nor is such ever likely to appeal to any but those in whom culture has developed the brain at the expense of the heart—wisely, perhaps, for themselves, but not wisely

for those who, subject to their example, are still un-
prepared for a purely logical code of ethics.

It is desirable, in the discussion of these things,
to avoid any statement that may sound like a judgment. It may be that pure science is the religion of
developed humanity in the future; it may be that it
will not do more than play protestant to the existing
Christianisms, purifying them and ridding them of
all that is not "sweetly reasonable"; it may be that
religion, deriving overwhelming strength from some
new prophet of God, may with a new revelation
sweep all our existing isms to Gehenna. Between
religion and science it is not attempted to decide;
but it is urged that each has its separate function in
the world, each addresses its own peculiar people
save where, thanks to a better balance between
heart and brain, they are both open to both. The
multitude is not intellectually developed; it does
not act by scientific rule; it is certainly to-day incapable of self-sacrifice in the general cause of humanity. The voice it understands is the voice of
authority that can quell or command the heart, or
the voice of tenderness that can touch and lead it.
For the teaching of virtue we must still fall back
upon religion—religion with its music, its ritual,
its flaming imperative, its kindling enthusiasm, its
note of praise and its hush of prayer.

He must be a great—or a rash—man who would
attempt in one lifetime to solve a problem that can
probably only receive its solution in the slow development of the race. The very education that has

made us critical makes us bad material for prophets
to work with. Were a Siddhartha to rise amongst us
to-day he would probably never step forth from his
harem; Christ would never return from the wil-
derness, and Mahomet would perish ingloriously in
the cave of Hori. It is not through the voice of
any one man that the religious question to-day can
receive an even approximate solution; but it is to
be hoped that through the slow ascendency which
man can acquire over his inclinations during generations of effort and conduct he will at last reach
a point where the ethics of science become coterminous with the ethics of religion.

That there are certain directions along which his
efforts may be more fruitful in the future than in
the past is likely; perhaps also there are fields of
labour which have been neglected heretofore and
which may richly repay culture and effort; perhaps,
even, there are strongholds of evil which exist rather
through our tolerance than through their strength,
and which will be found to have been a prolific
source of moral depravity, acting where we least expected and injuring where we felt most secure.
These are some of the practical questions which it
may not be unprofitable to study, and perhaps, to
some small extent at any rate, answer.

The object of the preceding pages has been to
show that religion and science are not destructive
of one another, but, on the contrary, join hands in
teaching substantially the same rules of conduct;
that each, however, has a separate and necessary rôle

to play; that religion appeals to the heart, science to the mind; that religion orders, science persuades; and that because humanity is an exceedingly complex thing, being composed largely of men who have hearts more open to the command of religion than they have minds open to the persuasion of science, religion, in spite of the defects in its creeds, has to-day a mission to perform which all should respect and support; that the scope of action which religion and science should cover probably requires readjustment; and that religion can be helped by a conscientious study of what it really is, and what it may, with increasing wisdom, become.

CHAPTER II.

PERFECTIBILITY OF MAN.

CHRIST said, " Be ye therefore perfect, even as your Father which is in heaven is perfect." Nor could he ask of us less than perfection. He started from a state of perfection; from the example set by an all-good as well as an all-wise and all-potent God; he came down from heaven and reascended to heaven; his mission to man was to fit man for a heaven not in this world but in the next. To demand perfection from man was consistent with his scheme of salvation; to demand any less would have been inconsistent with it.

The command of science is a very different one. Science does not allow us to aim at perfection, or even to hope for perfection. Its injunction is a much more humble one, and because more humble perhaps more practicable and less hopeless; it may be summed up in the word improvement.

Science, in asking for improvement, points to the history of man for encouragement; religion, in demanding perfection, could only derive from that history despair. Science demonstrates that step by step evolution has, by proceeding from lower to higher

24

types, stealthily but surely scored success; religion would have, on the contrary, to record an uninterrupted succession of failures.

It is well to set a high standard, but a standard is too high if it is beyond our range of vision as well as beyond our range of hope. This is the mistake that science avoids. It moves slowly from one known order of facts to another, from the development of the protozoön to that of the mollusc, from that of the invertebrate to that of the vertebrate, from that of the savage to that of the civilised; it argues that what has happened can go on happening, and because development has not, so far as we know, proceeded by leaps and bounds in the past, we have no right to expect that it will proceed by leaps and bounds in the future, though that it can be made to advance, and advance in the direction of improvement, seems to be indicated by the whole scheme of Nature as it becomes more and more unfolded to us.

Nor is there any conflict here between the dictates of religion and those of science. Religion, consistent with her rôle, deriving her language as well as her inspiration from the exaggeration of the East, overstates her case. Science, less dogmatic because less authoritative, proceeding cautiously from fact to fact, taking nothing for granted, fearing to err by claiming too much, hoping to attain by claiming little, understates. Thus religion tells us, if slapped on one cheek to turn the other also; if robbed of a coat to offer the cloak also. Science teaches the doctrine of resistance, inculcates justice, orders reparation.

Religion teaches us to despise the body and care only for the soul. Science answers, " *Mens sana in corpore sano.*" The ascetic who, yielding to religious temptation, outrages his body by too little love of it is to the eye of science as immoral as the *gourmet* who, yielding to his appetites, outrages his body by too much love of it. There are no lights and shadows in the teaching of religion. She loves to clothe her orders in set rules and commandments; she uses the imperative; she consents to no exceptions; she admits of no compromise. Science is less positive. She recognises the complexity of man, his transitional condition, the weakness of his body, the limitations of his strength. And yet both unite in enjoining the same rules of conduct : " Love your neighbour as yourself," and " Do unto others as ye would that they should do unto you."

Nor can we as yet dispense with the religious method even where it seems to depart most from common sense. Not only is every individual man a complex thing, but humanity is complex also. Ethical rules coldly reasoned out by science may be sufficient guides to philosophers; they will be *caviare* to the general. The uneducated must be treated with authority, they must be impressed by ritual, they must even be coerced by fear. Let, then, religion continue to do its work with those who cannot be reached by science, but let those who have outgrown swaddling clothes prepare themselves to stand alone ; let them recognise that perfection is not for our generation, and yet not in this recognition abate one jot of effort towards self-improvement; let them rather, by setting their standard within their comprehension and within the limits of human attainment, live up to it, and by the hourly effort of every day form character able to resist in the hour of temptation.

But to do this we must be clear as to what indeed constitutes our duty. We must be able to distinguish between science that is true and science that is false, between theories that are sound and those that are unsound; for if religion misleads us sometimes, science may mislead us sometimes also. There is no monopoly of wisdom in this world. We are all seeking light. We probably never see the whole of any ethical question. Our organs of ethical vision are not yet complete; in some of us they are absent altogether. We have the same consciousness of ethical truths as earthworms have of light. The whole of one end of an earthworm is sensitive to or conscious of light, and this consciousness enables him to grope to the surface of the earth, but he has no eye, he can distinguish no object. Just as the eye has developed from a mere sensitive surface, so our consciences have to develop from such dim notions of right and wrong as to-day confound as well as guide us.

Now it is believed that there are certain great principles which will, when recognised, help us in our efforts to improve the ethical sense; and having disembarrassed ourselves of the hopeless struggle to be perfect, it may be less difficult to recognise these principles, which, alas, are not consistent with such a struggle. So long as we are bent on nothing less than perfection, so long are we unable to recognise the limitations which make perfection impossible and the new rules of conduct which are consistent with those limitations. When we have learned to fly, then, perhaps, may we begin the attempt to reach the fixed stars; but until we have learned to fly we had best leave the fixed stars alone.

It has been necessary to point out the religious mistake of aiming at perfection; it next becomes necessary to relieve the ethical student of the paralysing doctrine so often taught by scientific men under the name of determinism; for it is an essential part of the question involved in the perfectibility of man to know how far, if at all, men are themselves factors in their own perfectibility. If, indeed, man is "an iron balance in which to weigh pleasure and pain," then there seems no room for ethical effort, no reason for ethical discussion, and we are left to the hopeless alternative proposed by Herbert Spencer—philosophic calm.

CHAPTER III.

DETERMINISM.

IF one thing differentiates man from beast more than another it is his conscious faculty to help on the forces within him that tend towards good, or to defeat those forces by yielding to the baser inclination. Physiologically man differs most from animals in the dimensions, the convolutions, and the efficiency of his brain; but this is merely a difference of degree—a question of more or of less. If we compare the lowest type of man with the highest type of beast, the difference becomes practically reduced to a faculty for speech and the use of tools; and these may result as much from the shape of the cavity of the mouth and from the digitation of the forepaws as from any great increase in the capacity of the brain. The essential difference between man and beast seems to consist in a faculty possessed by men to abstain from a present pleasure in order to escape a future pain. It is true that animals can be taught by man to do this very thing; but it is done by animals only through the education and under the eye of a human master; it is not believed ever to have been found in a state of nature outside of man.

Now this faculty of abstaining from a present pleasure to avoid a future pain, or of suffering a present pain in order to enjoy a future pleasure, is in one sense a direct development of the intellectual faculty, for when (as Huxley puts it) we learn the rules of the game, we find that physical well-being depends largely upon an exercise of this faculty; later we learn that moral well-being is no less the result of intelligent self-control; and so the determinists claim that the exercise of this faculty is only a form of enlightened selfishness, our own well-being constituting the end in view. And they are doubtless so far right. But there are two considerations which, as man develops, tend to complicate this reasoning, and these may be roughly named love and duty. For we have already seen that love tends to reach away from self—from the domestic relations, which are only a reflected form of self, to the tribe, the nation, and at last the race, self progressively becoming less and less until it reaches a vanishing point. And there grows up in the heart of man a new motive, called duty, which replaces selfishness by substituting therefor an abstract notion of right, to which we cling. and by which we conduct our lives irrespective of self, even in its remotest form. The determinists answer that this so-called love and duty are no other than pleasure in another form; that he who suffers pain out of love for his race (as Christ is believed to have done) or out of a sense of duty (as Socrates) is merely obeying the greater impulse, which is none the less a greater impulse because it seems to be an unselfish one. The maniac who destroys himself or the dervish who tears his flesh is the slave of an idea; in his case the idea is a false one. In the cases of Christ and Socrates the idea was not a false one, but it was equally an imperative one; it dominated its victims no less imperiously. In this sense neither Christ nor Socrates was free to do otherwise. The nobility or unselfishness of the dominant idea does not make it any the less the determining idea. Determinism is therefore as true of the patriot and martyr as of the criminal or debauchee.

Men who have grasped this argument tend to fall in love with their own perspicuity, and to regard with a feeling akin to contempt all those who cling to the unphilosophical convictions of consciousness to the contrary. To look upon the best part of humanity in its efforts to improve itself by defeating inclination and selfishness in compliance with the abstract rules of love and duty; to look upon this heroic effort as a part of the human comedy, a mere substitution of one idea for another; to regard its victims as "fools of Nature" pluming themselves as heroes in a paradise of their own imagining, while they are to the superior eye of the philosopher mere manikins with strings pulled by the greater inclination—this, to some persons, lifts them to the plane of the select and superior few, and seems to gratify, although it ought to humiliate, their self-esteem.

Against this tendency we must guard ourselves.

Reason may err as well as religion; dogmatism may
be a vice of one as well as of the other; and reason
alone may be as unfit to decide some of our problems as sentiment.   For the question before us now
is one of mixed fact and judgment.   We have not
facts enough to proceed to demonstration; we must
take the facts we have and reach our conclusions
from these facts as best we may, with the least inconsistency and the least assumption.   Unfortunately, one of the facts with which we have to deal
is a fact of consciousness, and for that reason the
most difficult of all facts to handle.   For a fact of
consciousness is one upon which different individuals do not agree.   To many the idea of a man being
free to do one thing rather than another seems absurd; nothing in their experience justifies it.   On
the contrary, a review of their own actions in the
past convinces them that, though they may at certain times seem to have chosen to do one thing
rather than another, they are convinced by the light
of philosophy that as a matter of fact they have
never done anything save what the greater inclination dictated.   Others are equally persuaded that
their decisions are voluntary and free; that there
are presented to them two courses, between which
they choose with deliberation and freedom, sometimes pursuing the course most in accordance with
their natural inclinations because they believe it to
be the proper course, sometimes denying themselves
the luxury of yielding to their inclinations because
they believe their inclinations to be contrary to their

highest duty. The determinists say this so-called freedom of choice is an illusion. The non-determinists retort that men born blind cannot discuss colour; that the absence of this faculty of choice in some does not justify these last in denying it to those for whom its existence is as certain as that of the world in which we live. And so the battle ineffectually rages, no convincing argument being possible between combatants one set of whom deny the very existence of the thing concerning which they are fighting, and the others of whom are bound to admit that the thing in question may exist only in themselves and not in those who deny it.

But need the battle continue to ineffectually rage? If each side ceases for a moment to strike at the other's demands and pauses to consider its own, will it not appear that both are right up to a certain point, and both wrong beyond that point? Do they not both claim too much? Can they not both abate their demands and come to a conclusion founded on common sense and truth?

In one sense, and perhaps it may be added, in a purely verbal sense, the determinists are incontrovertibly right—every man who adopts one course rather than another is following his greater inclination; if it were not so he would not have adopted it. This is so obvious that to contest it is vain. Let us take a concrete case: A man has to choose between jumping into an angry sea to save the life of an enemy at imminent risk to his own and seeing that

enemy drown before his eyes. No one is present.
In order to put human applause or censure out of
the way the scene may be laid upon a desert island.
If he allows his enemy to drown, the greater inclination coincides with the natural instinct of self-
preservation; if he saves his enemy, the greater inclination coincides with a notion of duty at war
with the natural instinct of self-preservation; but
it is no less for that reason the greater inclination.
This point must be yielded to the determinist.

But how did this notion of duty arise? To what
or to whom is it attributable? Can man contribute
to it in any way? Can education help it? And if
man can contribute to its existence, can he also contribute to its becoming at critical moments the greater
inclination? Can education do this also? Now, if
the determinists will admit that man can contribute
in the minutest degree to either of these things, then
he has conceded all that we, who believe in the so-
called freedom of will, need ask for; because, if man
can create his greater inclination, then he is not the
slave but the master of it.

This is the pivot upon which all ethics turn. If
man were the mere slave of his greater inclination
his ethics would be those of a whipped hound; he
would so conduct himself as to escape whipping; his
actions would be determined by what he believed
would conduce most to his pleasure and relieve him
most of pain. If he were intelligent and fortunate
he would be prosperous; if he were unintelligent
and unfortunate he would be unprosperous; his

prosperity would be mainly determined by the circumstances which surrounded him and his faculty for hoisting sail to favourable and trimming sail to hostile breezes. There is no future, no mission, no advancement for such a man beyond gratification of desire and escape from pain. This is the order of ethical sentiment which has brought the animal kingdom to the point where it now is—every race pitted against every other race—preying upon and being preyed upon. This is the order of ethical sentiment which has put man at the top of the predatory system, which has made of him the great carnivore, the destroyer and devourer of all living things, and yet himself also destroyed and devoured in turn by the meanest of the animal kingdom.

The consequences of such a doctrine are appalling. Amongst them may be counted the lesson to be drawn from evolution in the past as regards the life history of animal races. They have their rise and their fall; they grow from small beginnings to a certain point, and then they degrade and die. The race has its life history as well as the individual. The book of the world contains indelibly inscribed on its pages of stone the story of many a dominant and now extinct race. The age of the trilobite; that of the reptile; the stealthy appearance of the carnivora; their rapid growth sharply distinguished into quadruped and biped; the biped, by the development of his fingers, gradually calling to his aid that great factor in the development of man, the tool, and with the tool becoming master of all living things.

But the story is not finished; the same inevitable fate seems destined for man also. If the whole. history of creation in the past shows a gradual supplanting of one race by another, the triumph of one race corresponding to the extinction of another, the survival of the fittest involving the non-survival of the less fit; if there have already disappeared from the earth races which at one time seem to have ruled it, the Ichthyosaur, the Plesiosaur, the Machairodon; if to-day the great carnivora are rapidly becoming extinct, and man is left alone, with no animal to successfully contest his supremacy, what shall be the fate of man if left to the same blind forces which have brought him to his present place? Shall he not also in the end yield to another race? Is Huxley * not right when he says:

"The theory of evolution encourages no millennial anticipations. If for millions of years our globe has taken the upward road, yet, some time, the summit will be reached and the downward route will be commenced. The most daring imagination will hardly venture upon the suggestion that the power and intelligence of man can ever arrest the procession of the great year."

If Huxley is right—if a downward route is inevitable; if nothing can arrest the procession of the great year—then there is but little reason for any ethics beyond those of the whipped hound: *Dum vivimus vivamus; après nous le déluge.*

---

* Evolution and Ethics, Romanes Lectures, 1893, p. 36.

We cannot afford to allow any of these discouraging results of science to go unchallenged. Scientific men are apt to suffer from the near-sightedness which overtakes all persons confined to narrow horizons. Dissection of animal tissue, chemical analysis, and microscopic investigation bring the eye very near to the object examined. There must be an occasional step back. The fly on the dome of St. Paul's can judge as little of its architectural effect as the palæontologist of the destiny of man, when he coldly concludes, from the extinction of dominant races in the past, that man must in his turn be eventually extinguished also. Man differs from animals in many respects, but in none so much as in his faculty to advance or hinder the forces that work for or against his own development. In this respect he becomes himself a determining element in his own evolution. The question whether he can arrest the procession of the great year in his own case is one which depends in part, perhaps altogether, upon himself. Is not this alone an argument in his favour?

The whole destiny of man, then, seems to hang upon the answer we give to this question of free will; for if we are going to relegate ourselves to the determinist condition of the lower animals, then we must expect to share their life history, and be ourselves overtaken at last by the doom which has overtaken them. But if there is in man a power or force which can overcome fate; if he can escape the law of the greater inclination by himself making that greater inclination different from what it would otherwise be ; if he is himself the spirit of the earth, framing his own destiny, lord of his own inclinations, the master and not the servant of those forces in Nature which make for decay, then may the race be immortal, and man become what the gospels have faintly shadowed—Emmanuel, or God with us.

And so the question we have to answer is this : Has man made and can man make his greater inclination ? If he can, then he has a conscious and volitional part to play in his own development, and it becomes of vital importance to him to study and understand that part not only for his individual advancement, but for that larger ambition which includes all his fellow-creatures in the great work of relieving humanity from abasement and pain and lifting it into dignity and happiness.

CHAPTER IV.

DETERMINISM AND THE EVOLUTION OF LOVE.

HAS man, then, made, and can man by conscious effort make or assist in making, his greater inclination? The best answer to this question will be found in those actual cases in which he seems to have already done so. Most conspicuous of these, perhaps, is the amazing degree to which man has by conscious as well as by unconscious effort created for himself a new inclination in his relations to the female sex. The importance of this fact in the development of man cannot be too much insisted upon; for man stands alone among the great carnivora in the possession of the faculty of herding, jealousy between males as regards females being probably the principal motive which forces the other carnivora to their solitary life. The lion, the tiger, the gorilla never herd; the same savage qualities which make them dominant over other races make them also unfit companions for one another. The consequence is that they are deprived of the advantages both for defence and attack which less formidable animals by herding enjoy. But man has been able to hold his own against his carnivorous rivals

4 39

not by bodily strength but by mental ingenuity; and the same ingenuity which devised the tool for defence against the lower animals devised also a scheme of existence for defence against one another. The tacit understanding which obtains among herding animals as to the distribution of females, as to the sentry system, as to mutual abstention from injury to one another during the chase, becomes in man, through language, expressed and written down. The notion of property arises, and of property in woman as well as of property in chattels. The necessity of respecting the property of a man in his women through fear of punishment at the hands of the community acts at first automatically to create a habit of self-restraint as regards women that may be the embryo as well as the precursor of that sentiment which in its highest development we learn at last to call love. But as civilisation advances woman herself becomes a factor in the community. She ceases to be property; her consent becomes an element in the sexual relation; and it is soon discovered that understandings and laws, written and unwritten, are totally unable to predetermine and maintain marital relations. The failure of law courts to deal with this problem restores it to the individual. The duel in one country, assassination in another, vendetta in a third, horsewhipping in a fourth, are all tributes to the hopelessness of the effort by legislation to determine permanently in advance the sexual relations of two persons, each of whom is changing from day to day as to his needs, as to his aspirations, and as to those qualities of heart and mind which go to make up a good or bad husband or wife. And so by the side of the code of rules drawn up by the state there grows up a code of morals determined by the public sense of the community and largely left to the conscience of the individual. Indeed, as woman becomes more and more enfranchised, the necessity of protecting her from the pursuit of man becomes less and less, until at last, as in the United States, it becomes practically *nil.* The marriageable girl is thrown by the occupations now open to her into the very jaws of temptation out of which a century ago it would have been deemed impossible for her to escape; even amongst the wealthy she abandons the tutelage of her chaperone so early as to become almost at once mistress of herself; and although there remains in the community some prejudice against divorce, this sentiment is disappearing so fast, that with the existing tendency to make divorce easy it may be said that marriage has practically lost its once indissoluble character, and is in some States rapidly becoming little more than a time contract. As to the wisdom or advisableness of this no opinion is here expressed; the fact is noted as a fact, because it tends practically to restore men to that condition of liberty which prevails amongst lower animals, by altogether destroying the notion of property in women, which first rendered social existence possible, and by partially destroying the mantle of indissolubility which religion subsequently threw around

the sexual relation. And yet, whatever may be the
ultimate effect upon the community of the twofold
change, to-day, at any rate, men do not tear one another to pieces in their contest for female favours.
Women may travel from one end of the land to the
other without fear of molestation; and there has
grown up between the sexes a sentiment called love,
which in its highest sense has so little, if anything,
in common with sexual passion, that this last is becoming less and less a factor in the marriage rela-
tion.ʿ Indeed, there seems to be a growing sentiment
that in the selection of a wife the existence of desire
should be counted rather as a reason against selection than in favour of it, and that marriage should
be instigated by sympathy of heart and mind rather
than by that physical attractiveness which seldom
outlives the first moon of married life. Through
what an amazing cycle has humanity in this respect
alone passed! Starting from a condition in which
sexual jealousy played so savage a part that it tended
to consign humanity to the barbarism and dangers
of solitude, the race evolved the notion of property
in the female sex, which kept women chaste by
compulsion and men chaste by fear; then, came
religion, with its humanising and beneficent doctrine of indissolubility: "A man shall leave father
and mother, and shall cleave to his wife, and they
twain shall be one flesh." And at last woman,
by the gradual extension to her, too, of the blessings of knowledge and liberty, is asking that the
shrine in which she has been imprisoned be cast

down, and that she step forth mistress of her destinies also.

It is impossible to conceive a more complete inversion of the so-called natural order of things. In a state of Nature selection is determined by physical attractiveness alone; the female is subjugated as well as persuaded by the male; she is held bound to him by fear if not by inclination; the relation is a temporary one, and terminated by the maturity of offspring, if not before. In the human family, on the contrary, physical attractiveness is largely replaced by attractions of heart and mind, and tends to become eliminated altogether; violence has disappeared as a determining factor; the slavery of the woman, after having been once enforced by law, has been replaced by a cult which, if it can be said to deprive her of any rights at all, deprives her only of those which a sovereign abandons when he mounts the throne. The relation, after having been rendered permanent by every sanction of religion and of law, is now being relaxed, so that it bids fair ultimately to depend only on the constancy of that new quality of the human heart called love, which, because it has nothing in common with the old savage instinct whence it has sprung, may eventually be relied on as a basis for the institution of marriage, with infinitely more certainty than the ban of the church or the penalties of courts of law.

The foregoing considerations disclose with singular felicity the prevailing error that præ-anthropic natural selection, and the principles of evolution

which result therefrom, are still operating on the
human race. So far is this from being true, that
the principles of selection in Nature and in civilised
man are found to be diametrically opposed to one
another. In Nature, sexual passion is fierce, eager,
and temporary; in man, love, which tends more and
more to replace passion, is gentle, calm, and abid-
ing; the one arouses jealousy, the other inspires
faith; the one creates solitude, the other courts
society; indeed, so essential to civilisation is the
substitution of one by the other, that we may without grave error attribute to this substitution all that
makes man greater than the lower animals.

And now that the fact has been stated, what
conclusion is to be drawn from it as regards man's
conscious part therein? It must be conceded to the
determinists that so long as the fear of punishment
or love of approbation constituted the whole law of
chastity, the habit of self-restraint acquired was due
to no conscious effort. But in that large period of
quasi liberty that has for centuries existed, and of
almost unlimited liberty that now exists, can it be
contended by the most bigoted determinist that human effort has had nothing to do with the respect
and devotion which have replaced the passion and
lust of an earlier day? Our literature abounds in
stories of the conflict between love and duty; of the
triumph of the one, of the sacrifice of the other; and
while our hearts go out to Guinevere and Maggie
Tulliver, we know that it is their expiation that
makes them dear to us, and not their surrender. We

know that it is by resisting temptation, and not by yielding to it, that our high ideals of love have been framed. We are conscious that the tug of Nature is in the direction of surrender, and that it is by the supremest effort only that we sometimes resist. We know that society, conscious of the overmastering sway of passion over us, has surrounded our women with safeguards, has to the utmost diminished opportunity for temptation, and has created a public opinion the fear of which shall keep us in the hour of trial. We know that with the whole force of custom, of public opinion, of lack of opportunity fighting on our side, the old Adam is still strong enough in us to harry many a conscience and ruin many a reputation. And yet, notwithstanding all the wrecks of human happiness which the struggle towards a high ideal of love involves, we see a noble intention aiming at a high purpose and justifying the price paid ; for every woman who has suffered in patience to keep her soul unspotted from the world, has contributed to render possible that sentiment which has lifted woman from a convenience to an inspiration, from a houri to a wife. This is what human effort has accomplished. Can it nevertheless be said that man is still, and must always be, the slave of his greater inclination ?

And if there remain any doubt as to the effect of this pernicious doctrine upon the conduct of man, let us assume that two youths of similar temperament are subjected, one to the teachings of a determinist, the other to those of an advocate of free will. The former is taught that he is the slave of his greater inclination; that if an order of sentiment called duty or dignity or love happens to be stronger in him than caprice or pleasure or lust, he will obey the former and not the latter; but if the latter happen to be the stronger, he must obey the latter and not the former; that he himself has no choice, and cannot by effort affect the result. The latter is taught that although he is in one sense bound to act in conformity with his greater inclination, nevertheless he can by effort resist the evil and incline to the good, so that by virtue of his resistance he can create a faculty which will ultimately prefer the good and instinctively avoid the evil.

Which of these two is most likely to make a brave man? which most to advance the fight of humanity with evil? which to make the best son, the best husband, the best citizen?

To this doubtless the determinists will answer: We are not concerned with the results of logic. Hope of heaven and fear of hell may also tend to make good sons, husbands, and citizens; but we cannot for that reason believe in the existence of heaven and hell, such existence being unsupported by evidence and inconsistent with our convictions regarding equity and justice. We are driven by an unanswerable logic to the conclusion that every act of a man complies with his greater inclination. If any act seems not to so comply the error is in the seeming. The fact that he has so acted is incontrovertible proof that it accords with his greater inclination; he cannot act otherwise. Nor can he create his

greater inclination unless there be in him an inclination to make the effort to do so; and in such case
the inclination to make the effort is already the
greater inclination.

This brings us to a point where the meaning of
the expression greater inclination can be usefully
discussed; for a brief consideration of it may lead to
the conclusion that we are fighting only about
words.

The principle of the survival of the fittest is no
longer applicable to the development of man. This
principle has put man at the head of the animal
kingdom, but his ethical progress depends to-day
upon his ability to overcome the very qualities of
the ape and the tiger, the combination of which
made him superior to both—in other words, man is
now engaged in fighting the very elements of his
nature to which he owes his existing supremacy.
Civilisation is teaching man how to cease to be
savage, cease to be treacherous, cease to be selfish;
it is teaching him how to maintain his dominant
position over the beasts of the field, and yet to supplant selfishness by altruism, treachery by wisdom,
savagery by love. Man therefore finds himself perpetually standing, as it were, between two sets of inclinations, forever hostile, forever at war with one
another; one set which he owes to his savage ancestor, one set which he owes to wisdom and religion.
These two sets of inclinations are marked by an
almost constant characteristic. The former, or, as
they may be called, the primary inclinations, are

those which we instinctively follow; the latter, or
secondary inclinations, it takes an effort to prefer;
the former appeal to our passions, appetites, and desires; the latter appeal to our intelligence and conscience ; the former generally promise present satisfaction, the latter generally involve present pain and
only remote advantage. Now if there is one fact
more than another with which those who have
studied the forming of character are familiar, it is
that men who habitually yield to their primary inclinations become incapable, if not insensible, of those
that are secondary; whereas those who habitually
make the necessary effort to resist their primary inclinations gradually form what we term character,
or a habit of acting in conformity with the secondary or higher inclinations; so that the word character may be distinguished from temperament, with
which it is often confounded, by the fact that
whereas our actions are determined by two sets of
influences, those we inherit and those we make,
temperament should stand for the tendencies we
inherit and character for the tendencies we make.

And if there is one fact more than another with
which those who have formed their own character
are familiar, it is that the formation of character is
attended by unceasing effort. This effort in our
childhood is exercised mainly by those to whom is
entrusted the task of educating us; in adult years it
is exercised, if at all, mainly by ourselves. But to
deny that effort is the *sine quâ non* of all ethical
self-improvement is equivalent to denying that ef-

fort is necessary to climbing uphill. In both cases
natural obstacles are being fought and overcome;
in both cases the instrumentality—human effort—is
the same.

And now we are able intelligently to discuss the
meaning of the expression, greater inclination. To
the determinist the expression means whichever inclination ends by prevailing; to the advocate of free
will it means the inclination which has naturally
the greatest hold upon us. In the determinist sense
of the word all freedom is impossible. The Omnipotent himself was not free to abstain from creating
the world; the fact that he created it is to the determinist incontrovertible proof that he followed his
greater inclination in so doing. Had he refrained
from creating the world, this fact would have constituted incontrovertible proof that he followed his
greater inclination in so refraining. In both cases
he would still be the slave of his greater inclination. But this is absurd; we must find, then, some
other formula.

Acts of choice that give rise to this problem of
free will, involve the presentation of two alterna-
tives: one agreeable to the instinct, but not commended by conscience; the other disagreeable to the
instinct, but commended by conscience. It requires
no effort to adopt the former; it requires effort to
adopt the latter. If effort is exercised and the latter
course is adopted, it seems to result that the agency
which made the effort performed an act characteristically different from those acts which require no

effort but are the necessary result of habit or instinct. Necessity characterises the latter; choice seems to characterise the former. We have here an inclination on the one side great enough to determine action of itself were it not that there exists at the same time an inclination on the other side which, *aided by effort*, may become great enough to overcome it. In other words, it is the effort of the selecting agent which makes the ethical inclination greater than the natural one. It is the faculty by effort of making the ethical inclination greater than the natural one which has been termed freedom of the will. Now those persons who have this faculty and who exercise it are universally recognised as strong men; those who have not this faculty and who fail to exercise it are universally recognised as weak men. The strong men are those who are capable of advancing humanity; the weak men are those who retard it. To which of these two shall we decide to belong? We know that by effort we can increase our capacity to live according to a higher law, and that by abstaining from effort we shall inevitably diminish such capacity. If we mean to surrender, let us by all means adopt the comfortable hypocrisy of determinism. If we mean to fight, let us recognise that the merit does not depend upon the question of freedom, but on the effort which may determine our choice in the teeth of natural inclination; on the effort which beyond all things differentiates man from brutes, and advances him along the way to dignity and happiness.

Then shall we cease to divide inclinations into greater and lesser, but rather into natural and ethical; the natural representing those inclinations which we inherit with the ape and the tiger, the ethical those which we strive towards through effort enlightened by science and religion; the ethical being distinguished from the natural by the fact that the former involve effort, but lead to a higher and completer happiness, and the selection between the two constituting that large part of human activity which, as distinguished from instinct, has been dignified with the name of conduct.

CHAPTER V.

DETERMINISM AND COURAGE.

THIS subject cannot be left without dealing briefly with another human quality which illustrates with singular felicity the distinction between our higher and lower nature and one of the factors which has transfigured it—courage.

Courage, like love, has in the development of our ethical nature moved through a complete cycle. Like almost every quality of the human heart, it has its origin in the conflict of life. Animals may be roughly classified into those that fight and those that flee. The former, through the application of the principles of the survival of the fittest, gradually improve their offensive weapons, and with this improvement grows also self-reliance; and the courage that springs from self-reliance; the latter—that is, those that flee—gradually improve their apparatus for flight, and with this improvement lose their willingness to fight or the courage which once marked their earlier condition. It is probable that the ancestor of the horse, when handicapped for flight by the large foot which was indispensable to support him in the marshes which he inhabited, was provided with de-

fensive weapons of more destructive character than
the hoof upon which the horse depends to-day. If
he had, he doubtless possessed the courage to use it.
This courage he has lost with the necessity of it.
Danger to the horse suggests flight; it is only under
exceptional circumstances that it displays courage;
as, for example, when a mare is put upon the defence
of her colt. And here we see another phase in the
development of courage which illustrates Nature's
plan in providing animals with just the courage
necessary for the preservation of the race, or, to
put it in a less religious and more scientific form,
the automatic arrangement under which those animals survive which have the courage to preserve
their race without the courage sufficient to constitute foolhardiness. It would be folly for a horse to
battle with a lion. On the other hand, if a mare
were not furnished with sufficient desperateness to
face a lion in the defence of her young, she would
possibly lack the courage necessary to defend them
against innumerable small carnivora to which they
would in such case fall a prey. And so the courage
of a mother in defence of her young is notoriously
foolhardy, as in the familiar case of the hen defend-
ing her brood against a Newfoundland dog, who
could devour her and her entire progeny at a mouth-
ful. Courage therefore seems automatically adapted
in the lower animals to the service it has to render.
How little conscious or deliberate it is may be seen
from the reckless use to which the honey-bee puts
its sting when the hive is attacked, although the use

of the sting involves death to the bee using it. The
bumble-bee, on the other hand, which lives alone,
which has no hive or community to protect, and
whose fate is an individual matter, has no sting, and
therefore suffers no martyrdom for others. To attribute to the honey-bee a conscious sacrifice of life
for his community is to endow him with the virtues
of a Quintus Curtius. It is more reasonable to believe that he uses his sting without knowledge of the
consequence, and that his action is practically automatic. When in the course of development the
animal becomes more and more conscious, when his
actions put on more and more the air of deliberate-
ness, those of them which involve courage put on
more and more the natural language of rage or apprehension. The snarl of the dog contains in it
much more of the " I would " than of the " I will ";
it shares with the spit of the cat or the hiss of the
snake that element of warning which appeals to
the sense of fear in the intruder. So we find
courage or aggressiveness and fear or submissive-
ness combined in animals very much in proportion
to their aggressive and defensive apparatus, and
to the special need therefore as regards the perpetuation of the race.

Now it takes no courage in a lion to pounce
upon a kid; his courage is called upon only when
the animal disputing him is about his equal in
strength. Defence of self and of the community on
the one hand, and the satisfaction of hunger and
sexual passion on the other, are the occasions for

the exercise and development of courage. Those deficient in courage tend to starve and die out; but altogether the most beneficient tendency towards maintaining and developing courage in a race is the contest for the female, which prevents the weak or timid from reproducing themselves, and confines the perpetuation of the race to the courageous and the strong.

In this short review we find all the elements that go to make up the highly complex quality of courage.

We have the courage that springs from self-reliance in the lion.

. We have the courage that springs from the maternal instinct in the hen.

We have the courage that springs from the social instinct in the honey-bee.

In these three cases there seems to be no recognition of danger, because in the case of the lion there is none; in the case of the hen it is ignored; in the case of the bee it is probably unknown.

Next we have courage tempered by a sense of danger in the snarl of the dog and the hiss of the serpent.

Lastly may be recalled that ineffectual courage which makes the grizzly bear attack and often slay the hunter, though it already has a bullet in its heart; that final display of vitality which, when we observe it in human affairs sticking to an apparently hopeless task, we call foolhardiness, and, when contrary to our expectations we see it succeed, we call heroism.

5

It is difficult to analyse the courage of animals, because we do not know how large a part the consciousness of danger plays therein. One thing, however, seems to be clear, and this is that the more highly organised the animal the more its courage seems to be attended by ferocity. In other words, anger seems to be an ally, if not a servant, of courage. All of the great carnivora are fierce as well as brave. Ferocity attends almost all their activities; a sort of savageness even attends their wooing. Ferocity becomes temperamental; they hunt with ferocity; they fight with ferocity; and it is with ferocity that they make love. No wonder that man, who is the greatest of the carnivora, should inherit temperamental ferocity also. But ferocity and the social instinct do not harmonise. The wolf learns to keep his ferocity within bounds when he hunts in packs; and so man learned to control this instinct when he abandoned the solitary life of his ancestor in order to enjoy the advantages of social existence.

There then arose in him a conflict between the instinct of ferocity and the herding instinct, which until he became a deliberating animal was largely automatic. Exhibitions of ferocity against his fellows were punished by exclusion from the community; and as he became more and more dependent upon community existence the punishment of exclusion became more and more severe. Then came penal laws to exert a constant pressure on his savage instinct, and religion with its appeal to his superstition and to those higher qualities which have slowly developed therefrom. Gradually ferocity and its poor relation, anger, have been put under restraint, so that it may be said that in our social lives we seldom see exhibitions of either. These are reserved for the occasional hurly-burly of public excitement or the permanent shelter of the home.

What effect has this suppression of ferocity and anger had upon human courage? Has it increased, or has it diminished, or has it altogether changed in form? It is impossible to doubt that civilisation tends to destroy courage. The history of the Medes and Persians amply illustrates this fact. Nor could it be otherwise, for civilisation breaks down courage in a twofold way: in the first place, it diminishes and even extinguishes the occasion for its exercise; in the second place, it educates—that is to say, it increases that knowledge and apprehension of danger which seem to be so conspicuous by their absence in the lowest forms of animal life.

Side by side, however, with this tendency to destroy courage civilisation carries with it tendencies to enhance it, for though we are bound to restrain ferocity in our individual capacity, we are not bound to restrain it in our collective capacity. The wilful destruction of human life by an individual on his own account is punished by death, but if committed on account of his nation is rewarded by the highest honours and offices of the state. In other words, war, and the consequent necessity for the qualifications that go to make good soldiers, have maintained a special education of youth which has kept alive in the race that quality of courage without which the race might possibly have disappeared.

Religion, too, has played a large rôle in the maintenance in man of courage of the highest quality. The tenacity and principle that made martyrs in early Christian days, soldiers at a later period, and exiles in still more recent times; the tenacity and principle which to-day strengthen the heart to resist the superstitions of education, to confront the public opinion of the immediate environment, and boldly cling to a conclusion because it is sincerely believed to be conformable to truth—these tend to create in us a courage which, if not identical with that of our savage ancestors, differs from it only in qualities that redound to the honour and dignity of man. For this courage is indeed a different thing from that instinctive and unconscious sting of the honey-bee, which, had it been informed, would have entitled it to a martyr's crown. It differs from it in that it is fully aware of all the evil consequences that will probably result therefrom; it differs from it still more in that, so far from being instinctive, it acts in a manner diametrically opposed to instinct; it differs from it in that while the one developed without conscious effort, the latter has grown only through the continual, increasing, and often heart-sickening struggle of every day; for if any man shall tell us that his courage has cost him no effort, it may be answered that in that case it cannot be accounted to him as a virtue, for he inherited it from a savage ancestor; whereas, to those

who in humility admit the struggle it has cost them
to be brave, let the palm of true courage be awarded,
for they have created in themselves a virtue that
is human, and have not contented themselves with
qualities that they share with the lion and the ape.
But courage such as this not only differs from the
old in attendant consciousness of danger; it differs
also in this singular and valuable respect, that it can
act without the impulse of ferocity or the assistance
of rage. True, many men whom we cannot but
characterise as brave, summon to their assistance
the ancient allies of their despised ancestors. But
the bravest in the highest sense is the man who
without a ripple of indignation, but with the calm
and skill of a surgeon, uses the weapon to slay an
invader which, did circumstances exact it, he would
with equal composure direct against himself.

And so courage, like love in this highest sense,
has become transformed by human effort; from a
purely instinctive and brutal passion, it has become
a deliberate and elevating virtue; and this transformation has been effected not by yielding to
nature, but by refusing the natural and creating an
artificial impulse, so that there has been created in
man a new quality, true to his higher nature, tending to his highest happiness, and consistent with
that Godhead the attainment of which must constitute his highest mission upon earth.

But not only is it indispensable to recognise that
such transformations as those from lust to love and
from ferocity to courage, result from the effort of

man in his struggle against inherited instincts, in order to put an end to the paralysing tendency of the doctrine of determinism; it is also indispensable because the whole tendency of civilisation is to destroy the very qualities which itself has rendered possible. Love, under the baneful effect of wealth and prosperity, tends to degrade again into lasciviousness; courage into timidity and indolence. Nature is no longer fighting on our side. We parted company from her when we declined to obey her savage laws; when we resolutely ceased to employ the weapons with which she had armed us; when we refused to allow the weak to starve and the sick to perish. We have undertaken a battle of our own. It is to ourselves, our intelligence, our resolution, our unceasing efforts, that we must now look for our well-being. The *laissez-faire* principle must be abandoned, as also the doctrine that the future can be left to the automatic principles of evolution that in prehistoric times prevailed. Nature put us at the head of the predatory system, and we have undertaken, in the name of God, to destroy all the qualities that entitle us to remain there, and replace them by virtues diametrically opposed to them. This is not a season for rest or philosophic calm; it is a season for effort, that man may complete the evolution of a higher nature as much opposed to the natural man as the gospel of love is opposed to the gospel of hate.

CHAPTER VI.

THOSE who have read the widely diverging definitions of religion collected by Mr. Kidd in his work on Social Evolution and the definition given by himself, will not expect any excuse for devoting a chapter to the question, What is Religion? Nor is the collection made by Kidd in a remote degree complete. Few definitions of religion have received wider or more intelligent acceptance than Schleiermacher's, which makes the essence of religion to consist in the sentiment that we all have of our absolute dependence; or, indeed, Feuerbach's, which finds the seat of religion in desire; nor can Hartmann's dictum be overlooked, which holds that religion is due to the presence of pain and evil in the world; or Darmesteter's, which makes religion to cover all knowledge and power outside of the domain of science.

Mr. Kidd's own effort to define religion is not a definition, but a theory. To him " religion is a form of belief, providing an ultrarational sanction for that large class of conduct in the individual where his interests and the interests of the social organism are

61

antagonistic, and by which the former are rendered subordinate to the latter in the general interests of the evolution which the race is undergoing."

The argument upon which he builds his theory is briefly this: There is no rational sanction for the conditions of progress; they are too unjust to the majority for the majority to have endured them, unless it had been induced to do so by a sanction that was ultrarational. This ultrarational sanction is religion.

Mr. Kidd's theory is too ingenious, too modern, and too attractive not to deserve consideration. It is attractive because it seems to explain so much. There is no more pathetic thread in history than the uncomplaining patience with which the submerged classes have during long intervals of time endured their fate. That this should suddenly be explained by a new definition of religion is captivating, but that it is so explained is open to grave doubt. It seems much more likely that what Mr. Kidd has sought to explain needs no explanation. Horses endure the bit, slaves have endured the lash, humanity has endured despotism, the citizens of American cities endure municipal misgovernment, all for the same reason: sufferance is the badge of all our tribe; man and beast endure because endurance is easier than insurrection. That religion has done much to inculcate the doctrine of obedience and submission is undoubtedly true; but that religion is nothing more than a sort of counterpoise to revolt can hardly be admitted.

Religion is such a complex thing that all who endeavour to trace it to a particular sentiment or to confine it within the four sides of a definition are likely to err. We cannot refer it, with Herbert Spencer, exclusively to the worship of ancestral ghosts; nor, with Mills, to the "craving for ideal conceptions, grander and more beautiful than we see realised in the prose of human life." No man who has seen a fellow-creature stricken dead by lightning is likely to scout the theory that *primus in orbe Deos fecit timor;* and few are likely to be satisfied with the explanation that religion is no more than "an habitual and permanent admiration."

Religions have varied in the history of the world as much as political institutions. The obvious and natural way to arrive at a definite idea of religion is to consider what is common to all religions, and what therefore differentiates them all. The task need not be a difficult or a long one.

Religions have been concerned mainly with the effort to account for all that seems inexplicable in the world. Whatever altogether baffled explanation was set down as supernatural, and there was woven about it the fancies with which imagination loves to clothe mystery. As knowledge increased, much that was once deemed portentous yielded to investigation, and it is not unnatural, therefore, that all periods of active thought should be marked by increase in the domain of science at the expense of the domain of religion. It is this view of religion which inspired Darmesteter's definition of it. There are certain

subjects, however, which, because they are probably
unknowable, have been the common problems of all
religions in all times and places. These subjects are:
How did this world come into existence? what is it
for? what is man for? what is life? is there a life
after death? and last, but not least, the justification
of pain. Indeed, the problem of pain emerges as the
great subject of religious enquiry; for after the deification of all the forces of Nature, which seems to
characterise the first writings of most religions—as
in the Vedas and in Greek mythology—there generally survives the notion of a single First Cause or
Creator, who becomes the principal object of worship. The necessity of propitiating this one God
gradually leads to the attributing to him of perfection as well as omnipotence, and then there stands
out the awkward fact of pain for explanation. And
not only is pain itself difficult to reconcile with
creation by an all-good as well as an all-powerful
God, but the unequal distribution of pain is difficult
to reconcile with the notion of justice. Indeed,
this last problem touches man so closely that it
swamps every other consideration, and the whole
theological system seems to be constructed for the
express purpose of furnishing something that will
serve as a quietus on this subject. We find, therefore, grafted on to the pantheism of the Vedas a
triune God—Brahma the Creator, Vishnu the Pre-
server, and Shriva the Destroyer—the inconsistency
between the existence of evil and the omnipotence
of the Creator being slurred over by the incorpora-

tion of evil with God in a mystical and unthinkable
trinity. This is a pitiable makeshift to a mind accustomed to exact reasoning; but in matters theological the mind allows itself to be hypnotised by
mystical words, because it has to begin by admitting
that it is dealing with matters beyond its reach.
But this trinitarian compromise of the conflict between omnipotence and pain did not settle the injustice apparent in the unequal distribution of suffering in the world. So glaring is this injustice,
that Mr. Kidd finds in it a sufficient reason for
religion in itself, and makes religion nothing but an
irrational sanction for an otherwise insupportable
evil. Undoubtedly the Brahman priests, whose pre-
eminence over the other castes depended upon the
religious control they could keep over their fellow-
beings, felt the importance of furnishing a salve for
this dangerous and ever-menacing thought, and so
was evolved the notion of an hereafter, which could
compensate for the injustice of this life; and the
hereafter devised was an ingenious one, involving
a strange intuition and anticipation of the doctrine
of evolution which was to supplant it : The soul is
believed by the Brahman faith to have reached the
human stage only by passing through the bodies of
lower animals; it can complete its evolution by reincarnation in man and increasing knowledge, or it
can take a downward way by reincarnation in the
lower animals. This doctrine served a double purpose : it explained how happiness above the average in this life, if undeserved by human effort, could

be compensated by degradation in a future life, and how unhappiness below the average in this life could be compensated by advancement, or reincarnation in a more blessed form, thereby solving the problem of injustice as regards distribution of pain; and it served to induce men to effort, in order to better their condition in this life and the next.

There are, of course, a thousand points upon which the doctors of Brahma differed and disputed, but the central point in this faith, as indeed it must be the central point of every living faith, is this question of pain.

Buddha introduced no great innovation into this part of Brahman belief. He was essentially a reformer. He directed his efforts against the abuses which attended the power arrogated to itself by the Brahman priesthood, and against asceticism as a means of salvation, but his teaching is ethical rather than theological. He was not much concerned with purely speculative questions; his gospel was a gospel of effort. He taught that appetite and passion were to be attacked by continual resistance, by occupation in good works, by abstinence from evil thought, and by self-renunciation.

His teaching brings prominently to view the essentially dual nature of most religions—that is to say, the difference between theology and ethics.

These two must be carefully distinguished, for they have no necessary, though they have a natural relation to one another. Theology is concerned with speculative religion; ethics with practical religion. The one endeavours to settle the uneasiness of the mind, the other to determine rules of conduct. It is in the neglect to recognise the dual character of religion that most definitions of it seem to err.

Although there may be no necessary relation between theology and ethics there is a natural connection between them, for theology serves to furnish a motive for conduct. The religious motive for conduct almost invariably takes the shape of divine command, and religions vary chiefly as to the character of this command and its sanction.

The God of Israel differs from the Atma of Indian religions in many notable points. The Hebrew mind, richly endowed with imagination and reverence, seems to have arrived at once at a conception of an omnipotent Creator without passing through the pantheistic stages of the Vedas and of Greek mythology; but not being possessed with the force of self-reliance which made the Greek and Roman soldier invincible in his prime, it projected for itself a God upon whom it could lean and altogether depend. The Hebrew mind was not speculative; it was not concerned with problems of justice and pain; it was essentially practical; it wanted a religion that could help Israel to fight its enemies and conquer. Such a religion they found in Jehovah, a jealous God, for whom Israel was a chosen people, and who could overcome the enemies of Israel by violence, by miracle, and, if need be, by guile. Such a religion could, so long as the leaders

of Israel were gifted with the faculty of inspiring
enthusiasm and faith, achieve results that fall little
short of miraculous; but the moment the leader
failed and faith failed, the very fountain of their
success failed, and the history of the Jews therefore
becomes the history of a succession of failures. The
Jewish religion could by its very nature never become that of any other race. Christ dealt a death-
blow to the Jehovah of the Jews. The conception
of God the Father is as different from the conception of the jealous God of Israel as Vishnu the Pre-
server is different from Shriva the Destroyer, to
which he is opposed in the Brahman trinity. Christ
did for the Jewish religion very much what Gauta-
ma did for Brahmanism, in that he based the ethical
system upon its reasonableness rather than upon a
divine command—not that the divine command was
wanting in either case, but that reasonableness was
added to it. Moreover, for the harsh and even cruel
doctrines of the preceding faith was substituted exhortation to benevolence and love. But Christianity could not come into contact with the Greek
philosophy and Roman civilisation without becoming speculative, and therefore there was early added to Christ's teaching the formidable institution
which allied itself to the state under Constantine
and devoured it under Hildebrand. Upon the
vague threat of punishment to the wicked and the
vague promise of reward to the good, which in
Christ's mouth does not necessarily involve more
than the measure of happiness which agnostics al-

low to virtue and the measure of pain which agnostics allow to vice, was built a complex system of rewards and punishments in after life highly localised and specialised, heaven for one and hell for the other, the keys to both of which were held by the Church, and precise places in which were allotted for a price by priestly condescension.

Here, therefore, as in the Indian religions, we find the same imminent problem of pain answered in a somewhat different way : heaven and hell have replaced the Brahman doctrine of transmigration.

The most cursory consideration of Islam will serve to indicate that here once more we find the speculative part of religion still devoted to the problem of pain, but, with an insight perhaps superior to that of the Christian Church, the Koran deals mainly with rewards—hardly at all with punishments. Punishment enough is there in this life. A religion that was to be propagated by war and on the battlefield must not make death a possible entrance to hell. Nothing but visions of Paradise were to attend the dying moments of the faithful ; enough for him to have behind the spur of fate, and before a paradise of houris.

The religion of the Greeks and Romans has not been considered, because it was not of the dual character which seems essential to a complete religion. It could hardly be said to have constituted a religion at all, for it is only with considerable difficulty that we can find an ethical element in it, and certainly it was without a shred of speculation. It consisted in a poetic deification of the forces of Nature, the ethical tendency of which, if any, was to teach courage in war and respect for ceremonial institutions. The speculative problems of religion were discussed by philosophers quite outside of all relation to religion. It is undoubtedly due to this that philosophy is often confounded with religion. As a matter of fact, however, there is philosophy which is religious, and philosophy which is totally outside of religion, although they both tend to merge into one another. For example, the problems of the mind can be studied from a purely physiological standpoint, or they may be studied in their relation to that product of the mind itself, the soul. The physiological view is purely philosophical or scientific; the psychological view tends to become religious or ethical.

Ethics themselves are often confounded with religion, because they form so large a part of the religious domain; and yet, inasmuch as ethics consist of the science of conduct, and conduct is determined by state laws as well as religious commandments, ethics cannot be defined as exclusively a part of religion.

The foregoing considerations will serve to indicate that all the great and potent religions of the world have been concerned with two different matters:

First, theology—that is to say, speculation as regards matters not included in the domain of science; and,

Second, ethics—that is to say, determination of rules of conduct.

Theology tends to become confounded with philosophy, and ethics with law. Both differ from both in one essential characteristic. All matters that concern religion deal with what, in the absence of a better term, we may call the higher nature of man— that is to say, those qualities and motives in man which differentiate him from the lower animals. It has been already pointed out that man is not differentiated from the lower animals by the development of his intelligence. In this matter he differs from them only in degree; and the cave dwellers of prehistoric days probably differ from the troglodytes of the Miocene period in mental development but little, if at all. Man does, however, differ from them essentially in the fact that he is capable of self-control; that he can refuse himself present pleasure or suffer present pain from a motive called duty, which, however determining it may be, is nevertheless one which has come into existence largely through the efforts of man himself, and can, thanks to those efforts, become more and more a factor in his conduct.

This sentiment of duty has become evolved not only through ethics, but through theology. It is speculation regarding the mission of humanity which has confronted us with the problems of creation, of justice, and of pain; and it is out of the results of these speculations that there has slowly emerged a sense of responsibility, the dictates

6

of which have become grouped under one word—
duty. Whether, therefore, we regard religion from
its speculative or ethical side, we find it mainly concerned with the same class of subjects, in all of
which the divine element in man stands strongly
contrasted with that which is natural or inherited.

In the next chapter, on science and religion, the
exact relation between the divine and the natural
in man will be more exactly described. Before
attacking that subject, however, from the point of
view of science it may be well to point out that the
above effort to describe religion is carefully divorced
from any and all religious creeds. It is believed to
be as applicable to the agnostic as to the churchman, and is particularly addressed to that large and
cultivated class of men who are estranged from the
Church because of inacceptance of religious creeds
and yet abstain from agnosticism because of unwillingness to abandon religious ceremonial; who
are inspired with what in the above sense of the
word are the highest religious motives, and are not
forgetful of old and hallowed religious associations;
who, in a word, are without any outlet or expression of the religious impulse, which is confidently
believed to be more capable to-day of forwarding
the interests of humanity than when, divorced from
science, it kept the world shackled in the so-called
" age of faith."

CHAPTER VII.

RELIGION : THE SCIENTIFIC VIEW.

IT may seem an invasion of the domain of religion for science to undertake to define the difference between the human and the divine in man; and if science undertook to exhaust the subject and to leave religion nothing to say upon it, the objection would not be without foundation. But however inadequate science may be to describe and deal with the divine part of the problem in its entirety, assuredly it ought to have something to say regarding the human part, and enough regarding the divine to be able to mark the boundary between them. At any rate, this is all that will be claimed for science in this chapter.

It has been already pointed out that a study of animal forms has discovered an evolution in conduct which roughly keeps pace with evolution of function; and it becomes important at this stage of the enquiry to define our notion as regards what conduct comprehends.

Conduct cannot be confined to intentional or ethical actions, for these last shade into actions that are unintentional so insensibly that it is difficult, if not impossible, to draw any hard-and-fast line between them. Conduct must be defined generally as an adjustment of means to ends, and is as applicable under this definition to the random movements of the infusorium as to the delicately adjusted aim of a marksman. What is meant by evolution in conduct is, that there is traceable in the advance from lower to higher types a gradually increasing adjustment of means to ends. In the lowest forms of animal life there seems to be no purpose whatever in animal movements. Those of the infusorium seem to be determined not so much by any intention or instinct on its part as by stimuli in the medium which it inhabits. As function develops, animal movements become less and less incoherent, and the more coherent they become the greater the economy of the race; for the movements of the infusorium leads it as often into danger as towards food, and millions perish of exhaustion and starvation for the few that survive; whereas, in proportion as function develops, and movements become more definitely adjusted to the end in view, there is a corresponding economy not only in the energy of the individual, but in the fecundity necessary for the preservation of the race. The progress, therefore, seems to be from animals which are homogeneous—that is to say, without distinguishable functions and whose actions are incoherent—to animals which are heterogeneous—that is to say, which have more and more specialised functions and whose

movements are more and more coherent. Again,
we find indefiniteness of form accompanying inco-
herence of action. Thus, the amœba has no precise
form ; it can only move by changing its form, pro-
truding a part of itself in the direction it wants to
go, and then dragging the rest of it after. Other pro-
tozoa are mere shapeless sacks. Increased definiteness
of form, therefore, as well as definiteness of action,
attends development from the lower to the higher
order of being. In the same way periodicity marks
the higher forms of life, whereas it is quite absent
in the earlier forms. The aëration of the air in the
blood, and the movements of the blood itself in
lower animals, are the result of irregular movements
of the body in which there is no trace of rhythm ;
whereas in the higher forms of life rhythm attends
both—the air in the lungs is regularly renewed in
the continuous action of breathing, and the blood
is poured through the body by the rhythmic beating
of the heart.

As animals become more and more developed
there comes into being, and there becomes more and
more developed, a nervous system, which informs
them, by the sensations of pleasure and pain, as to
which actions tend to prolong life and as to which
tend to shorten it, so that it could be said with great
probability that the lower animals are induced by
sensations of pleasure to perform acts which tend to
prolong life, and are deterred by sensations of pain
from those acts which tend to abridge it. Even in
man it can be said that, as regards most of the func-

tions of the body, pleasure attends the normal exercise of animal functions, while pain attends excessive or defective exercise of such functions; though
it must be admitted that pleasure and pain are not
as determining factors in human decisions as they
are in those of the lower animals.

The next step we observe in the evolution of conduct is the tendency of both motive and action to
become more complex.   Compare, for example, the
vague movement of a worm towards the surface of
the earth under the impulse of light upon the anterior part of its body with the complicated movements of rapid flight which result in a deer from the
definite picture on its retina of a pursuing carnivore.
Or compare this last again with the elaborate action
of a judge's mind when charging a jury upon complicated facts that have been brought out by the
examination and cross-examination of conflicting
witnesses during a week's trial.   This complexity is
enormously increased by the rôle which consciousness plays in determining conduct, and above all by
that judgment and choice which follow after.   Danger to a doe suggests flight; but if the doe have just
dropped a fawn, a few bounds away will betray her
fear; but the pause and the anxious look back to
where the fawn lies will reveal the anxiety of the
mother; she will be torn between timidity and maternal love; and though timidity may prevail in the
doe, in other animals less able to defend themselves
the maternal love will stay and fight.   Here, then, we
find a new element involved—the element of judg-

ment; and this element of judgment is in some animals extremely well developed, as, for example, in the
dog, whose sagacity in selecting out of the dozen
dogs he meets on a day's walk which of them he
can afford to patronise, which he must placate,
which he may bully, and to which he must cringe,
is hardly surpassed by man himself. And this sense
grows with the occasion for it. When animals herd,
as has been already noticed, rules of social life have
to be agreed upon and obeyed; and as they become
more clearly expressed and more certainly enforced
there arise a totally new set of motives for conduct,
until at last a man's action becomes determined not by
the immediate impulse, but by a set of secondary
and even still more remote impulses, such as good
fellowship, religion, law, and respect for public opinion. And as pleasure tends to accompany the exercise of every function which is adjusted to its special end, if consistent with the maintenance of life,
the exercise of self-restraint on the suggestion of
these secondary impulses gradually becomes attended
by pleasure, and so the discipline which was at first
reluctantly accepted as a necessity ends by being
willingly adopted as a virtue.

Moreover, attending the evolution of conduct
is a corresponding extension of human sympathy,
to which reference has already been made in the
first chapter, purely self-regarding actions gradually
yielding to those which include others in the sexual, parental, and tribal relation, so that at last self
becomes a vanishing quantity in the cult which we

finally entertain for the whole race. This extension of sympathy is not an accidental attendant of
evolution. Were it not for the growth of parental
altruism, progeny would not be sufficiently protected
to survive; and as a highly organised individual becomes more and more dependent upon the support
and help of his fellow-creatures, society, like a species, survives only on the condition that every generation hands over to the succeeding generations at
least as much in the way of benefit as it received
from the last. Parental altruism, therefore, must be
extended to social altruism; for if it be not, society,
and, as a part of society, the individual, will perish.
Now social altruism—that is to say, the consideration for others which gradually results from the
necessity of men's accommodating to one another in
the social state—is no more than a compendium of
every virtue; for out of the exactions of social life
there spring first the necessity and next the habit
of self-control; and out of the habit of self-control,
guided and governed by the perpetual pressure of
social obligations, there result all those other virtues
which make social life possible, prosperous, and
happy.

In the foregoing sketch of the evolution of conduct the effort has been made to omit every statement that could give reasonable ground for controversy, and to keep within limits that would command
the consensus of all scientific men. But in order to
do this many debatable points have been a little
slurred, and to these points it will be necessary to

recur; but before passing to the discussion of them it is well to point out how conformable the main conclusions of the foregoing are with the ethical teaching of religion. Even Mr. Herbert Spencer is constrained to yield a reluctant and somewhat condescending acknowledgment of it.

"After thus observing how means and ends in conduct stand to one another, and how there emerge certain conclusions respecting their relative claims, we may see a way to reconcile sundry conflicting ethical theories. These severally embody portions of the truth; and simply require combining in proper order to embody the whole truth.

"The theological theory contains a part. If for the divine will, supposed to be supernaturally revealed, we substitute the naturally revealed end towards which the Power manifested throughout evolution works, then, since evolution has been, and is still, working towards the highest life, it follows that conforming to those principles by which the highest life is achieved is furthering that end. The doctrine that perfection or excellence of nature should be the object of pursuit, is in one sense true; for it tacitly recognises that ideal form of being which the highest life implies, and to which evolution tends. There is a truth also in the doctrine that virtue must be the aim; for this is another form of the doctrine that the aim must be to fulfil the conditions to achievement of the highest life. That the intuitions of a moral faculty should guide our conduct, is a proposition in which a truth is contained; for these intuitions are the slowly organised results of experiences received by the race while living in presence of these conditions. And that happiness is the supreme end is beyond all question true ; for this is the concomitant of that highest life which every theory of moral guidance has distinctly or vaguely in view.

"So understanding their relative positions, those ethical systems which make virtue, right, obligation, the cardinal aims, are seen to be complementary to those ethical systems which make welfare, pleasure, happiness, the cardinal aims. Though the moral sentiments generated in civilised men by daily contact with social conditions and gradual adaptation to them are indispensable as incentives and deterrents ; and though the intuitions corresponding to those sentiments have in virtue of their origin a general authority to be reverently recognized, yet the sympathies and antipathies hence originating, together with the intellectual expressions of them, are, in their primitive forms, necessarily vague. To make guidance by them adequate to all requirements, their dictates have to be interpreted and made definite by science ; to which end there must be analysis of those conditions to complete living which they respond to, and from converse with which they have arisen. And such analysis necessitates the recognition of happiness for each and all as the end to be achieved by fulfilment of these conditions.

"Hence, recognising in due degrees all the various ethical theories, conduct in the highest form

will take as guides innate perceptions of right duly
enlightened by an analytic intelligence, while conscious that these guides are proximately supreme
solely because they lead to the ultimate supreme
end, happiness, special and general." *

But Mr. Spencer does not make the conformity
between the teachings of religion with those of
science as great as it really is. He puts himself in
an attitude of hostility to theology, which is unnecessary and illogical. Though he may deny the
revelations of the " divine will," he too has to evoke
the " Power manifested throughout Evolution"; and
he cannot, by giving capital letters to the one and refusing them to the other, set his God above the God
of Christianity. The power manifested throughout
evolution is the God man has more or less ignorantly
worshipped since the beginning of the world. We
may fight about his manifestations, his attributes,
his personality, his laws, but never about his iden-
tity. We must all agree that there is no God but
one God; the question is, Who is his prophet?

Now several observations suggest themselves regarding the scientific explanation of the evolution of
conduct just concluded :
In the first place, it assumes that this evolution
has proceeded automatically from the beginning, and
can proceed automatically to the end.
In the second place, it slurs over the important

* Data of Ethics, pp. 203–205.

fact that pain and pleasure are no longer determining reasons for conduct in man.

In the third place, it assumes that evolution is as
applicable to civilised man as to savage brutes.

The untrustworthiness of pleasure and pain as
guides to action in man is met by Herbert Spencer
with the argument that these " anomalies " are " not
necessary and permanent, but incidental and temporary "; * that they result from the conflict between
the two moral natures adjusted to militant activities
on the one hand, and industrial activities on the
the other; that pleasurable and painful sensations
are fairly well adjusted to peremptory physical requirements. It is the emotional pleasures and pains
which are in so considerable degree out of adjustment to the needs of life. He sums up the subject
himself as follows :

" Mankind, inheriting from creatures of lower
kinds such adjustments between feelings and functions as concern fundamental bodily requirements,
and daily forced by peremptory feelings to do things
which maintain life and avoid those, which bring
immediate death, has been subject to a change of
conditions unusually great and involved. This has
considerably deranged the guidance by sensations,
and has deranged in a much greater degree the guidance by emotions. The result is that in many cases
pleasures are not connected with actions which must

* Data of Ethics, chap. vi.

be performed, nor pains with actions which must be avoided, but contrariwise.

"Several influences have conspired to make men ignore the well-working of these relations between feelings and functions, and to observe whatever of ill-working is seen in them. Hence, while the evils which some pleasures entail are dilated upon, the benefits habitually accompanying receipt of pleasures are unnoticed; at the same time that the benefits achieved through certain pains are magnified, while the immense mischiefs which pains bring are made little of.

"The ethical theories characterised by these perversions are products of, and are appropriate to, the forms of social life which the imperfectly adapted constitutions of men produce. But with the progress of adaptation, bringing faculties and requirements into harmony, such incongruities of experience, and consequent distortions of theory, must diminish; until, along with complete adjustment of humanity to the social state, will go recognition of truths that actions are completely right only when, besides being conducive to future happiness, special and general, they are immediately pleasurable: and that painfulness, not only ultimate but proximate, is the concomitant of actions which are wrong.

"So that from the biological point of view, ethical science becomes a specification of the conduct of associated men who are severally so constituted that the various self-preserving activities—the activities required for rearing offspring, and those which social welfare demands—are fulfilled in the spontaneous exercise of duly proportioned faculties, each yielding when in action its quantum of pleasure, and who are, by consequence, so constituted that excess or defect in any one of these actions brings its quantum of pain, immediate and remote." *

Mr. Spencer seems to have no doubts or fears about the future. In his mind the admirable mechanism which has brought man automatically where he is, will bring him automatically where he would be. The limit of evolution can be reached only in permanently peaceful societies,† and in that direction are we being by evolution slowly urged, until at last " there will disappear that apparently permanent opposition between egoism and altruism. . . . As, at an early stage, egoistic competition, first reaching a compromise such that each claims no more than his equitable share, afterwards rises to a conciliation such that each insists on the taking of equitable shares by others; so, at the latest stage, altruistic competition, first reaching a compromise under which each restrains himself from taking an undue share of altruistic satisfactions, eventually rises to a conciliation under which each takes care that others shall have their opportunities for altruistic satisfactions; the highest altruism being that which ministers not to the egoistic satisfactions of others only, but also to their altruistic satisfactions.

" Far off as seems such a state, yet every one of

---

* Data of Ethics, chap. vi.   † Ibid., chap. ii.

the factors counted upon to produce it may already
be traced in operation among those of highest natures. What now in them is occasional and feeble,
may be expected with further evolution to become
habitual and strong; and what now characterises
the exceptionally high may be expected eventually to
characterise all." *

Mr. Spencer does not in so many words say that
humanity can attain perfection without effort, but it
would be difficult to read the Data of Ethics without
concluding that this was Mr. Spencer's opinion ; and
it is submitted that no opinion could lead to more
pernicious results. Nor, indeed, is such a conclusion
inconsistent with the doctrine of determinism which
Mr. Spencer, in common with most scientific men,
professes. A philosophy the whole trend of which
is to make man the puppet of his inclinations and
the result of the same automatic agency that advanced animal life from the ascidian to the cepha-
lopod, cannot be redeemed by such a page as that
which closes The Study of Sociology, and bids us
" see how comparatively little can be done and yet
find it worth while to do that little : so uniting
philanthropic energy with philosophic calm."

But men of science are not agreed with Mr.
Spencer as to the possibility of man, as we know
him, ever attaining the condition of peace and
universal altruism which he describes. Evolution
is a very terrible process. It is too savage a concep-

---

* Data of Ethics, chap. xiv.

tion of creation ever to have been imagined by the mind of man. It is because the horrors of it are facts which unmistakably surround us on every side that we have been obliged to yield to it a reluctant acknowledgment. And one of the terrible facts of evolution is, that unless propagation is sufficiently great to create a struggle for life, degeneration sets in—or, in other words, unless a race perpetually produces more issue than can be accommodated, there will be no struggle, no privation, no misery, and therefore no selection; and the moment selection stops, not only advance stops but decay sets in. Evolution, like life, knows no compromise; it can exist only on the condition of activity. Rest is a prelude only to corruption.

This biological fact—the central fact of Mr. Kidd's book, and from the ghastly consequences of which he offers us no escape—if applicable to man could result in nothing but discouragement. Fortunately, it shares the same fate as Mr. Spencer's placid prospect. These blind processes of Nature are no more applicable to man, in the sense in which Spencer and Kidd would apply them, than are those of climate to a hothouse or the rustle of leaves in the wind to a church organ. But at this point we must take up the argument a little further back.

The progression from the lowest to the highest forms of life is given to us by the evolutionist as an unbroken series of logical and necessary sequences, some of the links of which may be lost, but all of which can with satisfactory assurance be inferred.

All these links are represented to us as bearing to one another the necessary relation of cause and effect; the forces that have been operating as having operated with all the regularity of law; the results as having come about with the certainty of fate; and, lastly, all these laws are assumed and discussed as applicable to humanity without mitigation or exception. And yet the fact is that, so far from each of them being the necessary effect of a known cause, they all rest suspended in space without any foundation in cause of any description; and at least twice, if not oftener, in the course of the series there has entered into the sequence a new fact equally uncaused and unexplained. In the first place, science has as yet furnished no explanation, and will probably never furnish any explanation, for the existence of force or matter. These have to be taken for granted. Unfortunately, scientific men—not all of them, but most of them—forget that they know no more about the origin of either or both of these than Topsy did about her own; and because they can trace a great deal about the evolution of force and matter they disregard the profound ignorance upon which all their subsequent superstructure is founded, and conclude as dogmatically as though they stood planted on a rock.

The next gap in their knowledge comes very soon after they have begun to trace the formation of matter into centres of order in the planetary system, for the appearance of life in the world is just as unexplained and baffling as the presence of force and matter themselves. But life probably existed in cosmos long before consciousness, and the advent of consciousness is again as bewilderingly unaccounted for as that of life or force or matter. And so, in spite of the beautiful regularity with which the laws of evolution do work, once we have reconciled ourselves to total ignorance as to the causeless coming into existence of force, matter, life, and consciousness, we must admit that, as regards these four (though it is possible that force and matter are one and the same thing, and we must say three, and not four) effect appears to be without known cause; in other words, so far as we know, these constitute exceptions to the law of cause and effect; and unthinkable though to our minds effect must be without cause, as regards force, matter, life, and consciousness, we must admit either that they are without cause or that we are so ignorant about the whole matter that we do not know enough to label our own ignorance.

Under these circumstances one would imagine that men accustomed to exact reasoning would be chary of denying a phenomenon of our own consciousness as clear as that which persuades us that we have the faculty of choice merely because such a faculty would add another to the list of unexplained events. One would imagine that they would be all the more chary of such a denial when they took into consideration the fact that the faculty of choice, if we have it, is a faculty of which we could have no knowledge except through consciousness, which is

itself as unexplained as consciousness itself.   Nor is
this hypothetical faculty of choice an insignificant
matter.   If it exists, it is the most portentous gift
that has been made to man ; it lifts him higher
above the lower animals than any other quality that
he possesses ; it lifts him not only above all other
created beings, but it makes him master of fate itself ;
in fact, it is the embryo Godhead in him to which
every religion has appealed, and in which alone lies
hope of his salvation.

This must not be considered as an attempt to defeat determinism by the hypothesis that man is possessed of a faculty of choice, based upon no stronger
argument than a datum of consciousness inconsistent with rules of logic.   Determinism has ceased to
have its paralysing effect from the moment that its
anathema on human effort was found to be nothing
but a word puzzle ; or, in other words, from the moment we recognised that, although to suit the forms of
logic we have to admit that we must obey the greater
inclination, we are nevertheless responsible and free
because we are able ourselves to make the inclination which we subsequently obey.   Nevertheless, it is
impossible to overlook the undoubted fact that some
of us are as clearly conscious of a faculty to choose
a disagreeable alternative over an agreeable one as we
are conscious of our own existence ; we are conscious
not that we have in the past by effort created a
greater inclination, but that we are capable now in
the present of choosing to act in accordance with a
less inclination, because we have a faculty—a special

faculty, different from anything else in the world—
by means of which we can violate the instinct which
favors compliance with the greater inclination, and
act in the teeth of that instinct against that inclination. Now, of this faculty we are as conscious as
we are of our own existence. The consciousness of
our own existence is not disputed, and yet it is entirely unexplained; it is as causeless as the faculty
of choice. If we have to admit the one, why not
bow to the same necessity and admit the other?

It is not necessary that all men should have this
faculty; indeed, it is extremely unlikely that all men
would at first have it. Consider how few men or
women would ever exert such a faculty! The vast majority of our fellow-creatures lead purely impulsive
lives; most of them are born with social impulses
which make them good fathers, brothers, and sons;
some of them are born with poor social impulses which
make them drunkards and incapable; some of them
are born without any social impulses, and these are
criminals. How many of them stand squarely before
a temptation the punishment for which is not in
sight, and refuse to yield to it? How many of them
have temperamentally bad tempers, and without any
reason save a sense of duty overcome their temper?
or are lascivious, and deny themselves? or are glut-
tonous, and abstain? In a word, how many lead
lives of principle and self-restraint without hope of
heaven or fear of hell, and with no motive save that
of dignity or self-respect? And yet it is these last
only who would be exercising this faculty of choice;

for it is of the essence of this faculty that it should
be exercised in the absence of such a motive as fear
or hope, which would in itself be sufficient to out-
weigh the attractiveness of the temptation.   In
other words, the attitude of the person exercising
this supposed faculty must be this: he must be
powerfully attracted by the temptation; it must be
one to which he can yield practically without fear of
punishment; he must be buoyed by no belief in a
future reward ; dignity and self-respect must in the
presence of the magnitude of the temptation seem
folly and nonsense ; and yet he must stand firm
and resist.   The man who does this has a faculty
which those who only resist in the presence of a
greater natural inclination or fear of pain know
nothing of, and concerning which, therefore, they
have no right to speak.

But the advent upon the world of such a faculty
is neither impossible nor improbable.   The *Ambly-
opsis spelæus* which inhabits the Kentucky cave
has no eyes ; if it were exposed to light, it is probable that the most adaptable individuals of the species would begin by experiencing a sensation on the
surface of a portion of their skin that would resem-
ble the anterior part of the body of the worm, which,
as has been already mentioned, is sensitive to light
but not capable of distinguishing objects.   Should
these individuals be able to communicate with their
fellows, how inconceivably difficult would it be for
them to convey the character of the new faculty,
with the embryo of which they were becoming en-

dowed. They would, in the first place, lack the idea
of light, which none could conceive save those who
were possessed of the embryonic faculty of vision;
they would lack words to convey an idea which
most of them could not conceive; and the very
vagueness of the sensation would contribute to their
difficulty, and to the contempt with which their
hearers would characterise them.

Such is the condition in which we are as regards
the faculty of choice. It is as unthinkable for the
majority of our fellow-creatures as light is unthinkable for those born blind; it is as causeless as consciousness; and it is an impertinence for one faction
of humanity to pretend to have a faculty that the
rest of humanity can know nothing about. And
yet this faculty is within the reach of all; it exacts
of us but two things: faith and effort. Not faith
in what we know cannot be true, but faith in what
we know may be true; not effort towards an ideal
we know we can never reach, but effort in a direction every inch of progress along which is so much
rescued from evil and so much gained in all time
for good.

And that "Power which manifests itself throughout Evolution," to which Mr. Spencer refers; that
Power which created the matter and the force, which
started evolution, which broke through the so-called
necessary chain of cause and effect, to bring into the
world uncaused life first, and uncaused consciousness afterwards, is just as able to put into the hearts
of men uncaused faculty of choice also; and He who

has manifested himself not only throughout evolution, but in the matchless lives of Buddha and Christ,
in the leadership of Moses, in the wisdom of Confu-
cius, in the fervour of St. Paul, in the poetry of
Shakespeare, in the music of Beethoven, and in the
frescoes of Michael Angelo; who to-day inspires
men to deeds of beneficence, whether it be one who,
swaying the destinies of a great empire, in the name
of justice abandons an easy victory over a weak but
exasperating foe, or, in the humble life of a sister of
charity, spreads the blessings of love in the strongholds of misery and hate—this Power has, since the
earliest dawn of light, striven to awaken us to a
knowledge of Emmanuel, or God WITH US. And
what is this God with us but the great faculty of
overcoming evil—which in our humility and weakness we have heretofore believed to be the exclusive
attribute of God himself?

Not outside, but within is the battle to be fought;
not outside, but within is the enemy; and not outside, but within, the conqueror.

Madame de Staël has said that religion was a
struggle, not a hymn. But with a strong belief in
our own Godhead, with a clear recognition that the
result depends upon our own efforts, with resolution
to continue the effort to the end, and with courage
to fight, whatever the odds, this struggling embryonic faculty which men deny to-day, will gain in
strength, in definiteness, in comprehension, so that
what seems now a struggle of discouragement will
end in hymns of praise.

And now having recognised that, though evolution does automatically proceed from cause to effect, its apparently necessary sequence has been broken in several notable instances, and having drawn pregnant conclusions therefrom, we have next to consider whether Mr. Spencer's explanation why pain and pleasure are no longer determining motives for man is a satisfactory one, and whether the principles of evolution are as applicable to man in the future as they have been to the lower animals in the past; for these two questions are intimately associated with one another—the answer to both resulting from the same as yet unconsidered fact.

Mr. Spencer recognises that the failure of pain and pleasure correctly to determine what ought to be the conduct of man is due to a conflict, but he regards the conflict as one between two moral natures adjusted to what he calls militant activities on the one hand and industrial activities on the other; and he considers the conflict a purely temporary one, destined to disappear in the era of peace, towards which evolution is directing us.

It is submitted that this is not an explanation. Mr. Spencer is generally so lucid, that the moment he ceases to be so we are startlingly aware of it. His standard is sufficiently high for obscurity which we should overlook in most writers to become conspicuous in him; it challenges our attention, and suggests that it is not a mere obscurity of expression but an error of thought. There seems no necessary connection between the confusion attending militant and industrial activities and the confusion regarding pleasure and pain. If evolution were proceeding normally from a militant to an industrial condition, there is no more reason why pain and pleasure should wrongly guide during this phase of development than through any other. The conflict which does effect this confusion in the working of pleasure and pain is a far more radical one, and, strange to say, one of which Mr. Spencer takes little or no account. It is nothing less than a conflict between man and the principles of evolution itself. In order to appreciate to the full this very opposite view of man's relation to Nature we must turn from the works of Mr. Spencer to those of Prof. Huxley. It is like moving out of an ice house into the open air. The ice house has its uses; there are to be found classified and scrupulously well arranged the corpses of every emotion or sentiment that have ever animated the human breast; nay, from the accumulated glaciers of geologic time have these specimens been collected and preserved for us, and there they lie dissected out for our examination and study, from the ancient religion that began with an ancestral ghost to the more modern philanthropic energy which lies congealed in philosophic calm. But after some weeks of this careful and edifying work we feel that we need the air, and this air we get in the breezy pages of the great agnostic.* For here man no longer figures as one of

---

* Prolegomena to Evolution and Ethics.

the millions of manikins slowly ground forth upon
a continually more and more heterogeneous plan,
over the workings of which he never had and never
will have any but a merely derisory control. On
the contrary, he appears as a combatant, instinct
with vigour and life, defiantly pitting himself against
the very forces of Nature to which Spencer tends to
regard him as hopelessly subjected. For man is
no longer mere plaster in the mould of evolution: he has taken to the business of moulding
himself; he has parted with ferocity and passion
and impulse, and has put in their place courage and love and self-restraint; he is studying
Nature as a chess player studies his board; he is
learning the moves of the destroyer and the answer-
ing moves with which they are to be met. Nature
is discovered to include two sets of forces: those
that make for life and survival and advancement,
and those that make for death and degeneration.
Man has undertaken by knowledge and by art to
put on his side the one and to counteract the other;
he collects his food from all the corners of the
earth so as to secure variety; he cooks it in order to
destroy dangerous germs and to reduce to the utmost the labour of digestion: he collects fuel in a
convenient form in houses of ingenious contrivance,
so that he can secure light, heat, and ventilation;
chemistry, physics, mineralogy, architecture, me-
chanics, and their allied industries, all help him in
his war against the hostile elements of Nature;
physiology and medicine fight disease; astronomy

guides his ships; the winds fill his sails; steam turns his wheels; the fitful flash of lightning is converted by his art into a steady illuminating glow; every useful force in Nature is turned to account in order to fight those other forces in Nature which are in his way. Ever conquering for himself new territory, he finds every new territory occupied by a new demon which he has to study and exorcise; he no sooner overcomes his ferocity than he becomes a prey to indolence, or conquers his indolence than he returns to ferocity; he no sooner enlarges his brain than he breaks down his body, or builds up his body but debilitates his brain; as the individual improves productiveness decreases, and the propagation of the race is left to less-developed types; and so, like a skilful fencer, he is forever advancing a step and retreating a step, seizing on his advantage here, covering a false attack there, but on the whole gaining and continuing to gain if he will only fight the fight manfully to the end.

And it is because man is fighting Nature that Nature no longer conveys to him by the simple though cruel warning of pain when he must leave off, or by the alluring message of pleasure when he may persist. He has created for himself an artificial habitation, where he must often endure pain that good may come and abstain from pleasure lest evil ensue; and it is this very confusion of pleasure and pain that is making him wise as well as brave; for knowledge, which at first was mere curi-

osity, has now become to him a dire need ; and courage, which he once directed only against his fellow-
creatures, he now summons to the daily conflict with
himself.

We can therefore subscribe neither to the quiet
assumptions of Mr. Spencer as to the automatic con-
veyance of humanity to the gates of universal peace,
nor to the dreadful doctrine of Weismann, that unless there is enough misery to create conflict and
selection the race must degenerate. Nor is it necessary to follow Prof. Huxley to the "procession of
the great year." What the future has ultimately
in store for the race no man can tell. What it has
immediately in store for us and for our children we
can tell, and it is our business to know. Those
who know this best will do best for themselves and
their environment. A brain to know, a heart to
love, and a soul to choose—these constitute the
equipment of a man ; and with this equipment he
need not fear to go out to battle with the world.

If, therefore, we revert to the original subject
of this chapter, as to what light science throws
upon the difference between the human and divine
in man, we have to distinguish between the teachings of different philosophers. We cannot rest on
the comfortable assumption that evolution is automatically doing the work of advancement for us ;
nor need we believe that there is no future for man
but one of perpetual misery and conflict. The plain
story of human life is not a difficult one to read if
we will approach the facts without bias or prejudice.

Man is a battlefield in which the forces of Nature
are at work in ceaseless conflict as in other animals;
but he differs from all other animals in this, that
he is himself a factor in the fight. Now all the
tendencies in him which he inherits from his savage
ancestors and which make against the social ideal
are opposed to those tendencies in him which make
for this ideal and have come into existence during
the struggle; it is to those continually opposed and
opposing tendencies that we refer when we speak
of the human and the divine in man. Were they
always sharply opposed in us, the difficulty of distinguishing them would not be great; unfortunately, so far from being sharply contrasted they often
merge into one another. We are like soldiers who
are called upon to fight an army a large part of
which wears the same uniform as ourselves; we cannot always distinguish our enemies from our friends.
Human qualities include not only vices that are
hostile to the divine—as, for example, passion, ferocity, selfishness, but also weaknesses that, without
being directly hostile, may through unwisdom or
excess become so. Hunger, thirst, sexual desire,
are all needs which require legitimate gratification;
the body cannot function at all without satisfying
the first two, and can probably not function at its
best without satisfying all three; and yet there is
not one of them that does not continually engage
us in a conflict which partakes of ethical character
and results in ethical consequences. Without, then,
endeavouring to enter too curiously into the ques-

tion, it can be broadly stated that every tendency or desire or effort that we share with the lower animals is human as contrasted with those with which they find themselves in conflict; and these last, because they are prompted by sentiments which in all ages have been termed religious, and because they are the evidences of the God in us, we call divine.

And here, at the risk of interrupting the logical sequence of the argument, it seems indispensable to point out that no effort will be made in these pages to deal with any problems of the remote past or of the remote future except in so far as those problems have a direct bearing upon our conduct to-day. This may seem defective to many religious people—and the word religious is here used in its widest as well as its narrowest sense—because they have been long accustomed to regard some of these problems as inseparably connected with both ethics and theology. Such problems as the origin of the religious sentiment, the immortality of the soul, and the future state are amongst those to which reference is here made. It may be contended at once that the origin of the religious sentiment has already been considerably discussed. So it has; but only so far as our knowledge of it in the past tends to contribute to the framing of rules of conduct for the present. The pretence of having in any sense explained how the religious sentiment arose in the human heart is here expressly disclaimed; and for an excellent reason—no less a reason than because no theory has as yet been given, and none can as yet be imagined that does ex-

plain it. How the faculty of choice—if such exists—
arose, is as little explicable as how the shapeless sac
of the protozoön developed into the complex organism man; how it acquired its senses, its organs of
vision, of smell, of taste. We can watch and describe
the process, but we cannot explain it. We have
in the end to refer it, as Herbert Spencer does,
to the " Power manifested through Evolution";
and reference to this unknown Power implies not
only the limits of our knowledge, but recognition
of a force superior to natural laws, and therefore
entitled to the name supernatural. Of course it is
possible that all that seems now supernatural may
with increase of knowledge cease to be so, and fall
within natural laws. But this future possibility
is not a resource upon which we can draw to-day.
We must admit to-day that we are wholly incapable
of explaining how there came into existence the
wonderful faculty of seeing with the eye, and the
still more wonderful faculty of seeing with the
heart or mind. Nothing can be more amazing than
this trinity of sense: the material organ of the
eye with its faculty of vision; the quasi material
organ of the mind with the faculty of imagination;
and the apparently immaterial, purely spiritual organ of the heart or emotions with its faculty of religion. Herbert Spencer may be satisfied with his
doctrine of ancestral ghosts; science may be satisfied
with the evolution of ethical synchronously with
that of physical function; but these are merely de-
scriptions of processes. Every effort to explain leads

us back necessarily to the unknown Power who has decreed that these things shall be as described, and who, working in the main along the line of cause and effect, is free to depart from that line, and has departed from it.

Religion, to many of us, and perhaps to the best of us, is the whole of life. Other things become dwarfed by its side; like grief, it becomes a "solemn scorn" of all things else. To these, the attempts of science to trace religion, to measure or define it, seem no less than a sacrilege. Nor is this sentiment without foundation in reason. When we are brought by calamity face to face with the cruelty of life there is no alternative but either to surrender or fight. If we surrender, we consign ourselves to a life of wretchedness; our wretchedness adds itself to the wretchedness of others, and we contribute to increase the pain in the world. If we fight, we join the ranks of those who have the hope and courage to believe that the human lot can by human effort be improved, and then we contribute to diminish the pain in the world. If we have suffered enough, this battle with pain, whether it be physical, mental, or moral, becomes overwhelmingly the most important work that there is in the whole of creation to do. Now, religion is the categorical imperative which sets us on to this work; and once engaged in it we can hardly suffer with patience the *dilettante* dandyism that sometimes characterises scientific enquiry into its origin. Reverence sets religion upon an altar; builds a temple about it; sacrifices to it the

pride of previous convictions; boldly proclaims it
supernatural, and drives from its shrine with indis-
criminate indignation philosopher, sceptic, and cynic
alike. Now, if we must bow to the supernatural in
the world, is any philosophy which pretends to ignore
it philosophical? Is not the temper that tries to
keep it in the background irreverent? Is not the
inconsistency that admits it in one page and denies
it in another sacrilegious?

And so, while the study of those facts which
science has marshalled to demonstrate the process
through which religious sentiment is evolved is in-
structive and necessary to an understanding of the
relation of religion to conduct, no attempt will be
made to deal with the inexplicable problems how religion came into the world, why man was set upon
preferring the noble to the ignoble, why he chooses
to do a hard thing instead of consenting to do an
agreeable thing. We *can* trace the gradual development of the religious faculty as we trace the
growth of the organ of vision in the animal kingdom; we can demonstrate its reasonableness; we
can show the ultimate advantage of ethical conduct
in the end; but here the mission attempted in
these pages ends. Pain is a fact; religion is a fact;
little is known of the past; nothing is known of the
future. But that religious effort can do something
to diminish pain is a conclusion of certain and incalculable value; and so whatever may have been
the origin of the religious sentiment, whether our
souls be mortal or immortal, whether there be a

8

heaven or a hell, the enhancement of the religious faculty must remain the one essential effort, and how this can be promoted the one essential enquiry.

What, then, is the outcome of it all?

As has been already, with perhaps wearisome iteration, charged, the salient, horrible fact of life is pain. But pain comes attended by a thousand ministers of love and consolation. That the life of charity, as St. Paul understood the word, is the life which, if followed by all, would most diminish pain in the world, cannot be doubted. That the life of charity can be consistently lived in this world of villainy and injustice is doubtful in the extreme. Life must therefore consist of a compromise between charity and self-defence, or, as Mr. Spencer would put it, between altruism and egoism. It does not consist in floating calmly on the propitious waves of evolution, nor need it be darkened by fears of the misery necessary to create selection; but it does consist of a conflict between the human and divine in us that is sometimes difficult, sometimes exhilarating, sometimes desperate. The man who hopes that religion can show him a royal road to perfection or happiness is like the camel that, having to climb a mountain, asked the way to do so across the plain. We must all strive to increase our knowledge so that the soul may know what orders to give the body, and the body be strong to carry out the orders of the soul; and we must strive to keep alive in us that faculty of choice or ability to create the greater inclination which makes us masters of ourselves; we

must be clear that it is by our own efforts that we
can work out our own salvation ; we must revere the
God in us, and the God in those around us ; we
must seek knowledge, health, courage, and reverence
—not any one, but all together—that a man may be
teres atque rotundus, with a wholesome mind, a
wholesome body, a wholesome, courageous, revering
heart.

When religion and science have come together to
make up such a man as this, then, perhaps, he may
be fitted to undertake self-government on that larger
field which, because it is larger, is for that reason
more complicated and more difficult, and yet upon
which every adult male is now at liberty to break a
lance in his own cause as well as in that of the
commonwealth—politics.

But before we enter on the subject of politics we
have still to consider the relation of the Church to
the state.

CHAPTER VIII.

THE CHURCH AND THE STATE.

Two recent books have undertaken to deal with the rôle which the Church has to play in practical life. One of them, penned in the cloistered seclusion of the university, unfolds with scholarly calm the history and mission of the Church universal; it handles the subject with love and reverence; it appeals to the reason and the heart of culture, and concludes in favour of the hope and belief that the Church is destined to increase its command over the consciences of men. The other, pounded out in the turmoil of the city, dictated hurriedly to stenographers during moments snatched from the absorbing duties of a publisher, prompted by the *sæva indignatio* of one who has seen vice triumph on the very steps of the altar, regarding Christ and the Church as mere pawns in his game, and in a rage to find that they do not prevent a stalemate, seizes that Church universal by the throat; reminds it that it is, or should be, also a Church militant; rates it for not usurping the duties of the state in the suppression of gambling, prostitution, and political corruption; threatens to create a rival civic

106

church which shall do what the Church militant has
failed to do; and closes with a chapter that antici-
pates time as well as victory in a description of
Chicago rid by his scheme of gamblers, prostitutes,
and politicians, and converted by a maritime canal
into a seaport, the capital of the United States and
the—hostess of the German Emperor!

It would be impossible to conceive of men more
different in temperament and education than Mr.
Lilly and Mr. Stead; nor would it be possible to
treat the same subject more differently than they
do; and yet upon one essential point they entirely
agree: both see and declare that the Church fails to
deal with the evils it was instituted to destroy, and
both seek a remedy. Mr. Lilly, after an able exposition of the superior claims of Christianity over
Buddhism and Islam, traces the influence of this
Church through the middle ages, the Renaissance,
and our own time. He points out that the history of
the world presents us with three distinct conceptions
of the relation of religion to human society: in
ancient times it was national; during the middle
ages it was universal; to-day it has become individual. The great and distinguishing peculiarity of
the middle ages is that in them throughout Europe
the whole structure of man's life, both public and
private, was built upon religion; and as there was
but one religion, and the Pope was the head of that
religion, the papacy constituted a power independent
of national lines, a spiritual kingdom—the Catholic
Church, with which Christendom was coterminous.

Guizot is quoted in support of this statement. " It is just at the moment when the Roman Empire is breaking up and disappearing that the Christian Church gathers itself up and takes its definite form. Political unity perishes, religious unity emerges." * To quote Mr. Lilly himself upon this point: " Hence Christendom, rather than the particular region of it in which they happened to dwell, was regarded as their true country and the first object of their patriotism. The rigid lines of de- marcation which in the ancient world had separated races, and had made the words stranger and ene- my synonymous, were broken down. The phrase ' Christian commonwealth' was a reality, and the several European states were sections of it. For the first time in the world's history, as a learned writer has well observed : ' we see not merely man, but humanity. The citizen and the helot, Greeks and barbarians, have disappeared, and in their place is a family of brothers, with one divine Father.'" † The Pope, too, according to Mr. Lilly, was the arbiter of Europe ; he was forever interposing between rival states and conflicting parties with the words of the leader of Israel, " Sirs, ye are brethren." The great injury which the Renaissance did the world was to break down the power of the Pope. From that period, what with the abuses in the Church denounced by Luther, the political

---

* Guizot. sec. xii. p. 230.

† Lilly's Claims of Christianity, p. 111.

secession of England, and the philosophy of Rousseau, religion has tended more and more to become a matter of individual conscience, less and less one of obedience and faith. But the legitimate consequence of separating Church and state is to restore to the Church the plenitude of her sovereignty in her own domain. In the exercise of that sovereignty it is inevitable that she should come into conflict with the state, for the two polities exist side by side for different ends though they govern the same persons. Marriage and education, for example, are obvious occasions of conflict, and the difficulty is increased by the fact that the new liberalism is to a large extent fanatically anti-Christian. But the principles of Christianity are impregnable; they alone can withstand the modern tendency to strengthen the state against the individual, and it is probable that in this new age " the office of the Catholic Church in vindicating the rights of conscience, the immunities of the city of God, will be of even more importance to mankind than in the primitive and mediæval ages. But we must ever remember that it is a new age. The old *régime* has vanished in the ecclesiastical as in the civil sphere. The intellectual conditions of life have changed as well as the political. And it is a grave question how far Catholicism has as yet responded to the needs of modern thought. Philosophy must expand in order to deal with the fresh problems raised by modern physics and modern metaphysics, collecting and collating the elements of truth scattered through

systems the most incongruous. To rear such a philosophical edifice is the great architectonic work lying
before us in the order of thought." *

It is not easy to understand how Mr. Lilly proposes to settle the conflict which he recognises must
be waged between the Church and the state on matters so fundamental as marriage and education, nor
how the story of the Church can be deemed complete
without reference to the check which the Church
put upon scientific research in the middle ages, or
the revenge which scientific research has taken on
the Church in recent days. Last, but not least, how
far, if at all, the Roman Church can " respond to the
needs of modern thought " without sapping the very
foundations on which she rests, must remain extremely problematic. That the Roman Church will continue to do its great work among those that profess her
creed must be the pious wish of all who believe that
a large part of humanity stands in need of the
peculiar kind of support and consolation which the
Roman Catholic Church seems peculiarly fitted to
give; that the movement of humanity is not to-day
clearly in the direction of progress all frank people
must admit; that Christianity does by the everlast-
ing truth of its morality keep man up to his fight
with evil must also be admitted; that the Roman
Church did in the middle ages contribute towards
the survival of Christianity as an institution even
Protestants may admit; but whether the Roman

---

* Lilly's Claims of Christianity, p. xxxv.

Church can ever recover its old international supremacy, or whether, even if it could, it is desirable that it
should do so, is more than doubtful. A large part
of the Roman Catholic population in America would
undoubtedly reject such a suggestion with patriotic
indignation; Protestants would combat it with fanatic rage, and all men of science would respond
to it with an emphatic No. In any conflict which
the Roman Church undertakes with the state in
America, whether on the subject of marriage or education, she will be hopelessly worsted. Nothing,
therefore, remains for her to do but to expand
her philosophy so as to make it " respond to the
needs of modern thought." When she begins this
work it will be time to discuss her ability to do so.
As yet we can but recognise that she does exert a
tremendous force upon the individual lives of men;
that she does take care of her poor, visit the sick,
and, through the angelic lives of some of her orders,
spread the blessings of loving-kindness amongst
men. That she may continue to do this, and by
modification of dogma may increase the number of
those whom she beneficially affects, is devoutly to be
hoped; but that her relations to the state and her
conflicts with the state may be diminished to the uttermost cannot but be desired by all who have her
interests most at heart.

Let us now close Mr. Lilly's book for a moment
and turn to Mr. Stead's. We must not allow ourselves to be shocked by the title of Mr. Stead's book
into the belief that for that reason it is worthless.

Mr. Stead knows nothing of the sentiment that pauses after pronouncing the name of Christ. But if reverence be conspicuous by its absence, there is no lack of discernment in its pages; they fairly burn with apostolic zeal, and the suggestions they contain demand our earnest study. Mr. Stead sees that religion has failed to do its work in Chicago; that "the churches, by insisting so exclusively upon the other life, have banished Christ from his own world, and by the substitution of divine worship for human service have largely undone the work of the incarnation." * He also sees with the keen eye of the practical man —and it is here that he strides far ahead of Mr. Lilly—that " the separation of religion from politics has enthroned Satan in the City Hall," and that it is only by restoring to religion its control over the public as well as the private lives of men that he can be driven therefrom. He sees that almost every social evil depends for its luxuriance upon the character of the local government; that almost every great problem with which our churches and charitable institutions are wrestling depends chiefly for its solution not upon the churches and charitable societies, but upon the faithfulness of our public servants; the problem of pauperism upon the wisdom and devotion of our charity commissioners; the problem of vice upon the watchfulness and fidelity of our police; the problem of education upon the impartiality and enlightenment of our school trus-

---

* If Christ came to Chicago, p. 14.

tees; moreover, all these officers derive their inspiration for good or evil from the mayor, who stands above them all. Mr. Stead sees that if religion is to do its work in our American cities it must take hold of local politics with a resolute grip, and his book is largely an exposition of this necessity and an exhortation to this end. The facts stated therein are familiar to every student of municipal government in the United States; they are not overdrawn—it would be difficult to overdraw them; the depth of degradation they reveal is appalling, but hardly more so than the indifference with which it is regarded by the citizens whose lack of civic sense is largely responsible for it. The question of municipal misgovernment will be treated in a separate chapter. What concerns us particularly in Mr. Stead's book is the method proposed by him to correct it, viz., the organization of what he terms a civic church.

In reading Mr. Stead's chapter on this subject we must learn to read without impatience that, in contemplating the evils rampant in Chicago, he "felt sorry for Christ." We must learn to excuse the inveterateness which insists on preserving the name civic church for the associations Mr. Stead desires to see formed for municipal improvement, although he admits that Cardinal Manning wrote him : " Call it anything but a church, and I am with you with all my heart; call it a church, and not one of my people will lift a finger to help you "; and although the Methodists were even more vehement in their denunciation of the term. We must get over our astonishment to find that this proposed church is to be "not only a place of worship, but a pleasant lounging place where the members may find any recreation they desire," and that it is to include "a large amusement hall, billiard and pool tables, checkers, dominoes, and other games, and stands for the sale of cigars, light temperance drinks, and lunches." All these things are the Salvation Army side of Mr. Stead's book, and not for that reason the least valuable to the student of the religions of to-day. We cannot afford any longer when our reverence is shocked on one side of the road to pass disdainfully over to the other. The Salvation Army is doing a great work upon the members of the army itself, if upon no one else; the methods it employs challenge our attention and respect, however distasteful they may seem. No one who has heard them defended by Mrs. Ballington Booth can fail to recognise that they have enlisted in the cause at least one woman of genius and refinement. The lesson to be learned from Mr. Stead's book is that the great evils from which humanity is suffering to-day are evils that can be handled only by religious sentiment; that the handling of those evils has been in great part surrendered to the state; that the state has itself been delivered over to corrupt political machines; that such machines are not only unwilling, but unable, to deal with those evils; and that nothing but a religious awakening of the citizens to their public duties can save countless millions from misery, and the state itself from degradation.

Mr. Lilly seems to think that the Roman Catholic Church may still prove able to overcome evil by enlarging its creed so as to respond to the needs of modern thought; and Mr. Stead, tired of waiting for this millennial day, proposes to run an opposition church on the lounging-place, cigars, and pool-table principle. Are either of these suggestions practicable? and, if not, where do they fall short?

The extreme danger of restoring the Church to a position which could precipitate her into conflict with the state has been already briefly referred to. In Anglo-Saxon countries such a proposition is too repugnant to require discussion. The Church is expected to act upon the conscience and conduct of the individual, but is also expected to abstain from all collision with the state. How, then, can the Church, as such, attempt to deal with political matters? and if the Church cannot do it, whence is the new Messiah to arise?

There is a deeper reason than one of mere policy for confining the Christian Church to its influence upon individual conduct, and the reason is obvious . enough. Christ aimed at no more; he did not attempt to deal with man's relation to the state except upon the memorable occasion when the Pharisees sought to ensnare him with the question, " Is it lawful to give tribute unto Cæsar, or not?" and with divine sagacity he answered, " Render therefore unto Cæsar the things which are Cæsar's; and unto God

the things that are God's." * Christ disappointed the
Hebrew hope that their Messiah would be a political
deliverer. His message was not to captive Israel, but
to captive humanity. Quite apart from the question
of policy, which alone would have sufficed to prevent
Christ from setting himself against the whole power
of the Roman Empire, the character of his mission
was essentially individual, not political; his whole
teaching is directed towards helping men to be lov-
ing and just towards one another; to eradicate evil
in its very source—the human mind; to prefer things
spiritual to things worldly. It constituted a morality
which every man was entreated to apply to his daily
life. Man's private conduct, not his public conduct,
was the object of Christ's concern. Nor is this
strange, for in those days man's public conduct
could call upon him but for a single virtue—obedience. St. Paul carries the exhortation to obedience
still further, for he contends that all temporal rulers
are heaven-appointed: "For there is no power but
of God: the powers that be are ordained of God.
Whosoever therefore resisteth the power, resisteth
the ordinance of God: and they that resist shall
receive to themselves damnation." † There is no
room here for the divine right of insurrection, but
only for the divine right of kings. Paul is unceasing in his exhortation to obey the powers that
be; ‡ nor does Peter refrain from a similar injunc-

---

* Matthew xxii. 17, 21.   ‡ Hebrews xiii, 17; Titus iii, 1.
† Romans xiii, 1, 2.

tion.* But if Christ abstained from dealing with public questions merely because his gospel did not include them, it is far otherwise with the apostles. To them and to the success of their teaching it was absolutely indispensable that no doubt should exist as to the purely religious character of their exhortations; hence the care with which obedience to the temporal powers is taught, and the charge of treason to Roman rule avoided.

How entirely different is the relation of the individual to the state to-day!

Throughout the whole of the middle ages—the age of faith—obedience remained the single rule that determined the relations of the citizen to the state. It was only at that period of the "breaking loose of human faculties" called the Renaissance that the virtue of yesterday became the reproach of to-day. Revolt and revolution stamp every page of history until the manacles which Church and State had put upon the minds and conduct of men were loosened. The sovereignty which had resided in the crown and tiara was shattered into as many fragments as there were citizens in the state possessed of the franchise. Government passed from the throne to the people, and the duty of the citizen changed from the exercise of obedience to that of authority. Is it possible to conceive of a more complete overturn?

And there is nothing in the teaching of the

---

* I Peter ii, 13, 17.

gospels, much less in that of the Church, to provide for this altered state of things. Nor has the Church been at all able to accommodate itself thereto. In many countries she has been dethroned and diminished. She has had to confine herself strictly to dealing with her parishioners in their private as distinguished from their political capacity. She has—to use the modern phrase—been obliged to " keep out of politics."

And not only has the Church been obliged to keep out of politics, but so also have all the institutions to which the Church gives rise—charitable societies, foundling asylums, orders, hospitals, homes for the aged. It is a pity that there cannot be added to this list the most important of all her institutions— parish schools. These, unfortunately, bring her into that " necessary conflict " with the state which Mr. Lilly confesses and deplores. At any rate, serious as this question of education is, it is clear that the Church is endeavouring to make its conflict with the state at this point as little felt as possible, and at all other points the divorce between the Church and politics is absolute.

Nor is this state of things confined to the Roman Church; it is necessarily the case with every Church and every creed. Even such purely lay institutions as the Association for Improving the Condition of the Poor, and the Charity Organisation Societies, have to steer clear of politics, and carefully insert a clause to this effect in their constitutions.

Now this holding off from politics has had a singular and subtle reaction not only upon the Church, but upon all who attend church. These last have become so accustomed to the idea that as churchmen they must have nothing to do with politics that they have learned to regard all questions concerning the state as outside of their jurisdiction; the more devoted they are to their Church and their Church institutions the more they abstain from taking any interest, much less active part, in political matters; so that abstention from politics has grown to be a sort of virtue, and, indeed, a matter of pride. Gradually all persons in office become regarded with some of the consideration which St. Paul exhorted the Romans to entertain for the powers that be, and churchgoers become resigned to municipal abuses in very much the same spirit as they became resigned to clerical abuses in the days of the Borgias. This tendency is enhanced by the fact that the Church and Church institutions are continually brought into contact with municipal officeholders, and generally in the relation of men who have favours to ask. Every Church is a landowner. The Roman Catholic Church is a very large landowner. Every owner of land is brought continually into contact with the city authorities in regard to such questions as assessments, improvements, sewers, police protection, and the like. In such cities as New York, where a *per capita* allowance is paid to religious institutions for those whom they support, this relation is intimate and apt to become collusive. Charitable societies are

9

continually called upon to confer with the heads of public charities, of prisons, of public schools. The necessity for this intercourse occasions a mutual disposition to be on good terms with one another; especially is this the case with those who are in the relation of suppliants for favour. There arises therefore amongst churchgoers and charitable people a notion that, however evil the city authorities may be, they are to be appeased, not fought, and, in the language of a contributor to the Charities Review, that more can be got out of them by co-operation than by resistance.

When, therefore, municipal abuses become too great for endurance, and the outraged citizen who is not a Churchman goes to the κάλοι κάγαθοι of the community for help to correct them, he is amazed to find that but little if any help can be expected from them. Clergymen very justly say that they cannot divide their congregations by introducing amongst them the sword of politics. The same answer is made by such bodies as the Young Men's Christian Association, by the managers of workmen's and boys' clubs—in fact, by every religious institution that has a pulpit or educational influence. But this is not all. The habit of tolerating municipal abuses and of conciliating municipal bosses has created a temperament which is perhaps a still more redoubtable enemy to good government than the enforced neutrality of religious bodies; for it is temperament that determines conduct, and it is from the conduct of her citizens that a city benefits or suffers. Now if the temperament of the best of her citizens is one of submission to municipal misgovernment and of aloofness from all matters political, then the salt has lost its saltness, and we may well ask, Wherewith shall it be salted?

Doubtless there enters into this apathy as regards the general weal a sense of property in a particular good work which absorbs the public spirit of those who succumb to it. One wealthy citizen of New York has a university in Chicago to which he devotes whatever millions he cannot spend out of his income; he therefore cannot subscribe a dollar to save his own city from Tammany misrule. Another gentleman has devoted himself to young men's clubs, and cannot allow his name to be associated with any political faction that might tend to diminish his influence in his clubs. Another has devoted himself to the rescue of children from the streets, and feels that all the time at his disposal is sufficiently taken up thereby. And so we are like a well-intentioned but insubordinate crew on an unseaworthy ship. Each one of us has attached himself to a particular leak, and will not hear of giving heed to any other matter, however much greater may be its importance to the safety of the ship. It is useless to point out to him that while he is sponging away a few comparatively harmless drops at the point to which he is devoting himself, tuns of water are pouring into a gaping hole in the ship's side. "That is not my business," answers the placid philanthropist; "I have only a limited amount of

time at my disposal; I cannot devote that time to
more than one point on this ship's surface. I have
associated my name and my personality with this
particular leak, which, you may observe, I am now
engaged in watching and staunching; I am attached
to it, and I flatter myself that it has become attached
to me. The task is an humble one; but I am not
ambitious. I know my duty better than you do, and
nothing—no, not the safety of the ship, nor your
safety, nor the safety of my fellow-creatures, nor even
the safety of myself and family—will induce me to
swerve from the task, modest though it may be,
which I have learned to consider peculiarly my own."

That this sort of self-righteousness and self-
regard has something to do with the abstention of
pious people from politics must be admitted; and
yet it must be regarded as symptomatic of the evil
rather than the evil itself. The evil itself lies
deeper down in the temperament created by a systematic reference to the Church as a guide in matters of conduct, and a systematic silence on the part
of the Church regarding that large part of a citizen's
duties which, now that he is sovereign, lie outside
of the Church, outside of himself, outside of his
home, in that public arena which has been cursed
by the name of—politics.

That this state of things should be disheartening
to those who are endeavouring to suppress a particular abuse at a particular time is not astonishing; but that it should be disheartening to those
who study these questions upon a wider horizon is

hardly possible. When an evil is the necessary result of a change for the better, there is every reason to hope that it will carry its own remedy with it. This is the usual course of development; and that the evil under examination comes within this category seems highly probable. A brief consideration of this question will not here be out of place.

Is the evil under discussion a necessary result of a change for the better?

When, on All-Saints eve, 1517, Luther nailed his ninety-five theses to 'the door of the Castle church at Wittenberg, he little knew, and the world little knew, what a revolution he had started; for by attacking papal authority he attacked all authority in its very stronghold. The Pope in his person represented the authority of the Church, and it was the Church that had held up the authority of every Christian king in Europe. It was but a step—and a very natural step—from the discussion of the authority of the Church to the discussion of the authority of the crown; and if ecclesiastical abuses had paved the way to the one, there were not wanting lay abuses to pave the way to the other. Abuse of authority brought its own remedy in state as well as in Church government. The same people that claimed the right of private judgment in matters clerical claimed it later in matters political; and so they overthrew the temporal as well as the ecclesiastical despot, and undertook the task of governing themselves. But here came the rub. It was an easy and delightful task to pull down the Pope and the king, but the setting up of a substitute was less easy and altogether troublesome. The task, therefore, which the people failed to perform was taken in hand by the few enterprising men who in every community know how to take advantage of the rest. The people did not awake, and has not yet awaked, to the responsibility it assumed in undertaking to govern itself. It seems a simple thing to cut out a cancerous growth; but the scar that is left behind is likely to give place to a hundred cancers in its place. The growth can be extracted, but not the disease. So the king who abuses power can be dethroned; but this dethronement of a king does not suppress the abuse of power for all time. The government has to be run, and governing involves the exercise of power. Somebody must exercise this power. The perpetual question for the people to decide is, Who shall exercise it? The difference between monarchical and popular government is not that in one case the monarch and in the other case the people rule. The difference is that in one case who the ruler shall be is determined by circumstances beyond the control of the people, and in the latter it is determined by circumstances within the control of the people. The privilege of the people, therefore, is not to govern themselves, but periodically to select those who are to govern them, either by making their laws or by executing them.

In order that popular government should work prosperously two things are above all requisite:

First, the people must be free to express their will at the polls; and, second, the people must be sufficiently enlightened to express a will that is wise and honest, and not one that is foolish or corrupt.

Now, if we take the second of these two first, it will not take long for us to decide that the people are not and could not be reasonably expected to be sufficiently enlightened to express a will that is wise on many of the subjects that are presented for their votes. How is it possible, for example, to expect that the mass of the people have sufficient information to come to a conclusion upon such a question as that of bimetallism, when experts cannot agree upon the subject themselves? How much more is the subject complicated when consideration is taken of the fact that a large part of the people is debtor to the other part, and the debtor part is told, however wrongly, that silver legislation will facilitate the payment of debts! or when the whole commercial class is told, however wrongly, that stagnation in business is due to insufficiency of coin in circulation! The same is true as to the question of free trade, or the purchase of railroads by the state, or the referendum, or single tax, or, indeed, all the other complicated questions of social and political economy that are periodically presented for their decision.

That the people are not sufficiently informed on these subjects no one can doubt. But, strange to say, it is not upon the decision of these questions that popular government has proved most disappointing. It is a matter not only of astonishment, but of great encouragement, that the popular decision has, on the whole, so far corrected itself where it has made a mistake that no great harm has resulted from it. The point where popular government has most notably and grievously failed is in the administration of municipal government, and this is due mainly to the fact that the people are not free to express their will ; and here we are brought back to the first of the two requisites for prosperous popular government above referred to.

Consideration of this subject leads us to the study of municipal misgovernment, as to the exact cause of which too careful attention cannot be given.

CHAPTER IX.

MUNICIPAL MISGOVERNMENT.

PRACTICALLY all citizens of the United States are members of the Republican or the Democratic party. There occasionally arise groups independent of both these parties in various parts of the country; but for many years these groups have hardly reached the proportions of a national party, and for the purpose of this discussion, therefore, we may divide all citizens into Democrats and Republicans. These national parties cannot exercise their functions without an extensive and elaborate organisation. They have to hold national conventions for the purpose of nominating candidates for the presidency and vice-presidency of the United States; they have to hold State conventions—that is to say, a convention in each State—in order to nominate candidates for election to Congress and State offices; and they also hold conventions in every city for the purpose of nominating candidates for the municipal offices therein. These conventions are attended by delegates duly elected at primaries or meetings to which all voters belonging to the party are admitted; and for the purpose of securing a sys-

127

tem for holding such elections each party has an organisation in every electoral unit. The number of
these electoral units may be measured by the fact that
in New York city alone there are no less than eleven
hundred and forty-one election districts, each election district polling between two hundred and fifty
and three hundred votes. There is in every election
district some one person, called the captain of the
district, whose business it is throughout the entire
year to keep in touch with the members of his party
in that district and to bring them to the polls on
election day. This means the employment of a vast
number of men and the expenditure of vast sums of
money and time. The fact that the population of
the United States is more and more forsaking the
country to congregate in cities makes the cities
more and more important in the game of national
politics; and not only do the cities represent a large
voting population, but city offices and city employment furnish a large amount of the patronage or
spoils upon the hope and distribution of which party
success to a great extent depends.

Now, it is not reasonable to suppose that the
mass of citizens who are absorbed in the occupations
of daily life can afford the time to do the hard work
necessary in order to play a rôle in party organisation. The party cannot afford to deal with ama-
teurs—that is to say, with men upon whose perseverance and punctual attendance to their duties it is
impossible to count. The result of this is that the
party machinery has necessarily fallen into the hands

of professional politicians. This is particularly so in cities, where the large number of offices and employments to be filled on the one hand, and the large number of applicants for such offices and employments on the other, furnish the conditions most favourable for the development of the machine.

It has been already pointed out that every party organisation requires the use of money. This is too obvious to require explanation. The necessary result of it is that every organisation goes more or less into the business of money-making; and the dominant organisation—that is to say, the organisation in any given city which controls the offices—ends by making money on a very large scale. It is quite unimportant to which of the parties this organisation belongs. In Philadelphia the dominant ring has for many years been Republican; in New York it has been practically always Democratic. It is the ring which belongs to the dominant party in a city that secures office, and maintains itself in power through the patronage and spoils thereof. But there are two sets of offices in every city—the offices in the gift of the city proper and those in the gift of the Federal Government; these last are considerable. In New York, for example, there are the offices and employments which belong to the extensive and complicated machinery of the post office, customhouse, internal revenue, and Federal judiciary. As the Federal Government is continually shifting from one national party to the other, it frequently happens that the Federal offices are in the enjoyment of one

machine, while the city offices are in the enjoyment
of the other; this keeps alive in every city two rival
machines, one of which tends to remain permanently
in the city offices, and the other of which comes
irregularly into the possession of those that are Federal. Thus, in New York, Tammany, the Democratic machine, remains pretty constantly in power
in the city, whereas the Republican machine only
enjoys office when the Republican party is in power
at Washington.

Now these rings are in politics for "what there
is in it," and for nothing else. The people and
amateur politicians may take interest in the national
issue, but the professionals take interest only in securing office. The natural consequence of this is
that the political leaders find it more to their advantage to come to an understanding with one another
than to fight one another; and so the tricks and ex-
pedients with which they are familiar on the race
course and in the prize ring are naturally introduced
into the political arena. The devices resorted to are
numerous; for example, the nominating machinery
being in their hands, they can agree to put up a
weak candidate for an office which one of them
agrees to surrender to the other; or they can agree
to pass the word round on election day that a particular candidate is to be scratched—that is to say,
his name scratched out of the ticket. An illustration of this may be cited in the campaign in New
York of 1888. Hill was in that year running on
the Democratic ticket for Governor of the State;

Cleveland was running on the same ticket for the presidency. The Republicans ran Harrison against Cleveland for the presidency, and Warner Miller against Hill for the governorship. It is openly stated and generally believed that the leaders of the respective machines entered into the following agreement—or as it is termed in the language of politics—"deal": The Republicans agreed to sacrifice Warner Miller to Hill provided the Democrats would sacrifice Cleveland to Harrison; this was called "trading" the governorship for the presidency. Three interesting observations are to be made regarding this election: In the first place, Hill is a notoriously corrupt machine politician; Cleveland has always stood for independence and uprightness. This "deal" had for effect, therefore, to defeat a good candidate for the presidency and to elect a bad candidate for the governorship. In other words, "deals" are never effected for the benefit of the community, but only to its prejudice. In the second place, the treachery was committed in the most corrupt districts of New York city and Brooklyn; that is to say, it is in the bad city districts that these arrangements are carried out. This is demonstrated by the vote cast therein, the story being told in the fact that Democratic tickets were voted with the substitution of Harrison for Cleveland, and Republican tickets were voted in which Hill was substituted for Warner Miller. In the third place, it is to be observed that Tammany is not in the least concerned regarding the national issues or party principles to which it belongs. Cleveland represents those issues—not Hill; for the President has in his veto the determining voice in moulding the policy of his party, whereas a governor is comparatively seldom called upon to take action upon a matter involving national issues. To sacrifice Cleveland to Hill, therefore, was to sacrifice the national issue for the spoils of local office. Now this is what Tammany stands willing to do at every election, and yet nothing exceeds the patriotism of its professions or the appeals to party loyalty in its manifestoes. Unfortunately, the citizens of New York have shown a lamentable willingness to believe in the one and to respond to the other.*

Another favourite method of carrying out deals between party machines is through the constitution of so-called bipartisan boards. It is a favourite theory of machine politicians—and one to which, unfortunately, intelligent and sincere citizens often adhere—that the departments of the city should be run not by a single responsible head, but by a multiple board of commissioners divided equally between the two political parties. This plan obliges a division of the spoils between the two parties to whatever extent it is admitted. It might seem as though the Democratic ring would object to a plan which

* See, for an example of this, the enormous majorities which the Tammany ticket received in November, 1892, because it was headed by Cleveland, whose election it had defeated in 1888, and whose nomination it had done all in its power to defeat only three months before.

would oblige them to divide offices with the Republican machine, but as a matter of fact Tammany is interested in keeping alive a corrupt machine in opposition to itself, lest haply in the absence of a corrupt opposition there should arise an opposition that was not corrupt, and that could, by the confidence it would inspire, bring together and keep together the real majority in favour of clean government that must exist in every city. Nothing would be so disastrous to Tammany in New York as the disappearance of the Republican machine. Indeed, it may be said that the Republican machine has contributed more to the maintenance of Tammany in power than all the boasted organisation of Tammany itself; for whenever the better wing of the Democratic party or a citizen's committee has put up a candidate who could command the votes of all good citizens, the Republican party has seldom failed to put up another candidate good enough to divide that vote and thus secure the election of the Tammany candidate.

Moreover, if there were no corrupt Republican machine with which to " trade," a large part of Tammany's strength would be withdrawn from it. Hence the willingness of Tammany to divide offices with the Republican machine to an extent sufficient to keep it alive, care being taken that the division be not sufficient to permit of its becoming dangerous.

The sources from which political machines derive money are numerous. For example, every can-

didate for office is called upon to pay an assessment
for his nomination in the first place, and for his
election in the second. The assessments paid to
Tammany Hall are officially known to have been
extremely large.

It is needless to point out that judges who owe
their election to an organisation which demands
and receives a cash price therefor can hardly be
counted upon for unbiased judgment where their
political organisation or its prominent members are
at stake. Another considerable source of income to
the machine is to be found in the contributions of
large corporations who seek thereby and get what is
called protection. In some States, where the machine is not as well organised as in New York, corporations have in self-defence to pay large sums in
bribery to individuals in the Legislature. The risk
and trouble attending this have caused corporations
in New York very willingly to accept the plan proposed by Tammany Hall and the Republican machine, under which, by paying large subscriptions to
these two organisations, they receive protection from
adverse legislation in Albany. As the organisation
owns the members of the Legislature which it elects,
it can deliver their votes for or against a measure
upon payment of a commensurate consideration.
Large contributions are also obtained by the organisations from all those persons whom they have to
employ, such as contractors, auctioneers, etc. The
worst development of this money-making system is
to be found in the assessment levied by the police

on gamblers, swindlers, and prostitutes; the black-mail levied by the city departments on all persons who sell goods, whether wholesale merchants or street venders, for so-called obstruction of the side-walks; that levied upon builders for privileges to which they are sometimes entitled, and for toleration to which they are often not entitled; that levied upon all persons who have occasion to violate the excise laws, the health laws, the tenement-house law, the laws on adulteration, and other laws passed for the benefit of the community, thereby putting those en-trusted with the execution of these laws in direct complicity with the violators thereof, and the police upon a corrupt and vicious understanding with the very criminals they are appointed to suppress.

It would seem that such an odious form of gov-ernment as this could not resist the indignation of its citizens. A very brief consideration, however, will serve to show that the very character of the evil is one which makes it extremely difficult to overcome. There are about twenty-eight thousand places of employment and offices in the gift of the city of New York. This means that the organisa-tion can count upon twenty-eight thousand votes directly, and indirectly upon those of thousands of persons connected by blood and friendship with the persons who enjoy these offices, and again upon many thousands more of those who are kept in the hope of succeeding to their places. The criminal and quasi-criminal classes, which are in complicity with the police, vote, of course, in a body for their

10

protectors. Every man engaged in sale, whether merchant or street vender, every builder, plumber, liquor dealer, has an interest in placating a power that can persecute him by overscrupulous enforcement of the city ordinances. The large corporations contribute to both political parties, and remain unwilling to fight either. The large army of contractors, contractors' employees, and men who have business relations with the city swell the number of the ring's adherents. Not only is this number large, but it is compact; it is held together by the strongest of human motives—self-interest; it attends carefully to its political duties, and implicitly obeys the orders of its chief. The discipline is perfect; the organisation matchless.

So much for the factors that go to make up the strength of the powers for evil. When, on the other hand, we turn to the consideration of those factors in the city which ought to be counted upon for opposition, we find them, in the first place, absolutely unorganised, separated by private and social interests into almost antagonistic cliques, and, above all, divided into two hostile political camps by the rivalry of opposing national parties. They are without any nominating machinery except that of the national parties to which they belong, and it is only under conditions of the most extraordinary exasperation that they can be induced to act irrespective of these parties. Indeed, only once, until last year, in the whole history of New York has this been accomplished, and this only after the ring had defied the city by admitting the wholesale robbery of which it was guilty, and asking the insulting question, " What are you going to do about it?" Temper had probably as much to do with the defeat of the Tammany ring in 1870 as public spirit.

But if we study this deplorable state of things in connection with the circumstances which led up to it, we shall have to conclude that it is a necessary phase through which our experiment in popular government had to pass ; and, like every malady of this character, it must end by purifying our Government or destroying it. Which it shall do, what are the chances for and against, and how, if at all, we can by efforts of our own determine the result, are enquiries full of the profoundest interest for us all.

It was a necessary phase through which we had to pass, because, when the heroic period of revolution was over and our ancestors were no longer buoyed up with the exhilaration of heroic action, the return of every man to his daily duties became not only a rule but a virtue; there was no voice raised to remind him that in shaking off the Government of England he had assumed the government himself ; and that if he abdicated, another ruler, as arbitrary, and perhaps less respectable, would mount the vacant throne; there was no religious duty upon him to perform his public as well as his private duties; there was as yet no abuse to gall once more the withers so lately galled by England ; and so the public fell into a profound political trance, from which it has not yet

awaked. It is idle to say that the occasional excitement of the people at election time can in any sense
be considered deliberate political action; they are
kept in a state of permanent hypnotic trance by the
confusion of national issues and the din of party
war; they see the motions of political life proceeding
before their inactive senses; primaries called to elect
delegates to conventions; conventions meeting and
talking; candidates nominated; processions and brass
bands; speeches and torchlights. Then, when election day comes they are aroused enough to get driven
to the polls; they are given a Hobson's choice between two sets of equally unfit candidates; they dis-
gustedly deposit their chosen ballot, or throw both
away and return to their political eider down. The
whole game is really being played for them, and they
are mesmerised into the notion that they are playing
it themselves.

For what, as a matter of fact, does take place?

The national parties, with their respective hench-
men, call primaries; nobody attends these primaries
but professional politicians*; professional politicians
therefore dictate who shall be delegates to the conventions. The delegates who attend conventions are
instructed by their chiefs and nominate a candidate
selected by their chiefs. The people therefore have
nothing to do with the nomination of candidates;
the only time when their intervention is asked or per-

---

* Article on Primaries by A. C. Bernheim, Political Science
Quarterly, March, 1888.

mitted is on election day, and then only to deposit
their ballot for one of two equally objectionable candidates.

It occasionally occurs that one of the parties finds
it advantageous to put up a candidate who stands
well in the community; the dodge is often a successful one, because such a candidate attracts all the
votes of those who want good men in office irrespective of party. But when the candidate gets into office
it soon becomes clear that, whatever his previous
record has been, he is in office for the benefit of his
party and its chiefs, and not for the benefit of the
people.

And so it has become inevitably impressed upon
the minds of the people that voting on election day
is practically a farce; that whoever be the candidate
proposed for their votes, and whichever be the candidate selected, it is the machine only that profits by
it. Hence a growing tendency on the part of the
public to abstain from the polls altogether. It is
practically only in presidential campaigns that personal fitness enters into the selection of the candidate; and this is due not to the inclinations, but to
the wisdom of political leaders; for the national
chessboard is such a large one that machines abstain
as much as possible from nominating candidates for
Federal office whose records will not bear examination. Public opinion when collected from the vast
territory over which a presidential election is held is
too great a force to be defied. Citizens therefore preserve an interest in presidential campaigns; they

feel less at the mercy of the machine, and are generally given candidates of such good personal character
that the choice is determined by the political questions involved. This is as it ought to be. But in
local elections hope deferred has succeeded in making
the heart sick. Abstention from the polls is believed
to be an indication of indifference; it is much
rather an indication of discouragement and despair;
for to cast a vote for a candidate who is known to be
unfit for office, or for one who, though personally fit,
is practically certain to serve as the mere cat's-paw
of the party which puts him in office, is repugnant
not only to common sense, but to self-respect. It is
probable, therefore, that those who abstain from voting on election day include the most deserving as
well as the most indifferent. Our citizens have still
to learn that the mere casting of a vote on election
day is an idle formality unless preceded by the efforts
necessary to secure the nomination of candidates
worthy of our votes. Voting is the last of our political duties; organization the first.

The hold which national parties have upon municipal politics is still more subtle than has yet been
made to appear. Election for State and national
offices taking place upon the same day as election for
municipal offices, the names of all the candidates
have to be presented upon the same ballot. There
are so many offices to be filled that the ballots are extremely complicated, and anything that serves to increase the confusion of the voter serves to diminish

the chances of the party which is the occasion of this
confusion. It has become, therefore, an axiom with
practical politicians that it is indispensable to be able
to offer a voter an entire ticket which he can, without complication or confusion, deposit in the ballot
box, free from the necessity of manipulating it himself by the addition or erasure of any names.

Now, if any effort is made in any city to bring
together those men who desire good municipal government irrespective of national politics, and they
put up candidates for municipal offices without at
the same time putting up candidates for State offices,
they cannot put a complete ticket into the hands of
the voter. If they only put up a ticket containing
the candidates for municipal office, there is put upon
the voter the necessity of combining the ticket of
the municipal reformers with the ticket of one of the
national parties; and experience shows that this involves the voter in trouble and confusion to which
he is not willing to submit. It follows, therefore, that
none but the most conscientious and enthusiastic
supporters of the municipal reform movement will
vote a reform ticket; the mere trouble of adding or
subtracting a few names or adding a few pasters is
sufficient to deter the mass of voters from the use of
an incomplete ticket. And yet, on the other hand,
the municipal reformers cannot put a complete ticket
into the hands of the voter, because this would involve putting up candidates for the State and national offices, thereby occasioning the very confusion
between municipal and national politics which they

have particularly set out to avoid. The only remedy for this is for municipal elections to be held at a different time from the national and State elections. This would not only render possible a purely municipal ticket, but it would also facilitate the possibility of organising municipal associations for the purpose of improving municipal government by separating municipal government from national politics; for the moment it becomes possible to put a purely municipal ticket in the field it removes one of the principal objections that national partisans now have to such organisations. To-day they decline to join such nonpartisan organisations because they fear to be put in opposition to their own parties by the conflict which yearly arises in the making up of the ticket; for, as things now are, national parties put into the field a ticket covering municipal as well as State offices, and, as has been already shown, they have many reasons—mostly bad—for so doing. But if an election is purely municipal the national parties have no excuse for putting up a municipal ticket, no national issue being involved. If they do, they invite defeat at the hands of their own partisans; for, at any rate, the issue will then be fairly presented as between partisan and nonpartisan candidates, no citizen desiring good government being any longer under compulsion to vote a national ticket for fear of sacrificing a national issue. Much importance, however, cannot be attached to this reform until those who want good municipal government are persuaded of the importance of organised municipal parties to that special end, and are willing to undertake the special trouble and expense of constituting and maintaining them. Many efforts are being made in various cities of the States to do this very thing, but the movement is still in its infancy.

Another direction in which national politics exert a baneful influence upon our citizens may be observed in the practical certainty with which efforts at organising associations to reform municipal politics are sure to split, at some time or other, along the line which separates the Republican from the Democratic party. Over and over again indignation has brought citizens together for the purpose of resisting the vicious despotism under which they live, only to break to pieces the moment a committee is constituted, because partisans in the committee endeavour to use the committee for partisan ends. The result of this is that either the committee breaks into two parts and then its work practically comes to an end, or one faction in the committee overcomes the other faction, and then the support of the beaten faction is practically lost to the reform movement.

There is still another hold which the national parties have upon our municipal affairs. Cities have a very small measure of local government. The board of aldermen have in many cities reached so low a pitch of degradation that they have been gradually shorn by a jealous Legislature of all their powers, and the city is governed not by its board of

aldermen or council, but by the Legislature of the
State. New York is thus governed by Albany,
Chicago by Springfield, and Philadelphia by Har-
risburg. It not infrequently occurs that a measure
of the most vital municipal importance is defeated in
the State Legislature because it falls into the hands
of a majority from the country which is entirely
ignorant of municipal needs. So also it not infrequently happens that the State majority belongs to
a different national party from that of the city
officers, and then these two engage in perpetual war,
one against the other, the Legislature legislating
officers out of office and endeavouring to control the
city against the wishes of the majority therein.

But perhaps the most serious element in this
control of the Legislature over cities is to be found
in the fact that, so long as the cities elect members
to the State Legislature who are to have a voice in
making laws for the cities, it becomes essential for
all organisations constituted for the purpose of municipal reform to put up candidates for the Legislature. Now in so doing they directly interfere with
the national parties, for State matters are entirely
in the hands of national parties, and the members
of the Legislature are called upon to legislate for
the State as well as the city. Moreover, it is the
members of the Legislature who constitute the elect-
ors for the United States Senate. Every member,
therefore, of the Legislature is an object of interest
to the politicians at Washington; so that national
parties cannot in their own interests abstain from

intervening in the nomination and election of members of the State legislatures; nor can those who are interested in the welfare of the city abstain from so doing either.

The above considerations serve to show the considerable difficulties that stand in the way of the organisation of associations constituted for the purpose of rescuing city government from national politics, and inferentially, therefore, the difficulty of breaking down existing abuses in municipal government.

Nor is it to be expected that the national parties will ever willingly surrender their hold upon municipal politics. Cities offer too much in the way of spoils for national parties to be willing to dispense with them. Those who do the routine work of politics for national parties must be rewarded, and national parties have practically only one form in which to make this reward—office. Now, the leaders of national parties, those men who, by their intelligence and temperament, deserve the first prizes in the State, are drawn away from the political mass to Washington; but the humbler workers—those who do what may be called the dirty work of politics, who love politics for its excitement, for its freedom from regular duties, for the comparatively large rewards it offers for small service, for the character of the service itself, and the personal consideration which attends it; all those men who haunt liquor saloons and places of amusement and disreputable

sport—these are kept at home in our cities, to corrupt and govern us. As a matter of fact, national
parties have heretofore regarded municipal office
only as strongholds of patronage, rewards for party
service, or occasions for political traffic. They interfere with municipal government only to corrupt it.

As has been already observed, some people are
of the opinion that city officials are not all as bad as
is pretended, and that more can be obtained in the
way of municipal improvement by co-operating with
these officials than by resisting them. In the words
of a recent contributor to the Charities Review * :
" Under our existing political conditions, experience
seems to show that more can be accomplished by
the quiet, intelligent, and well-directed efforts of
individuals, and of such organisations as societies for
city improvement which do not directly antagonise
those who wield political power, and which receive
the approval of the general public, than by spasmodic movements for reform." This view is so
largely entertained that it is worth while throwing
upon it the light of some actual experience. Let us,
therefore, briefly review some of the efforts made in
this line in the city of New York during the immediate past, and draw from them their lesson.

One of the defects in our municipal government
in New York, which is most felt by the citizens be-

---

* Charities Review, Archibald Welch, On the Sanitation
of the Dwellings of the Poor, February, 1893.

cause it is the most obvious, is the failure to clean
the streets. For some years prior to 1892 a group
of the ablest citizens in this city endeavoured by
co-operation with the city officials to improve the
city government in this respect. It is not necessary
to more than mention the names of James C. Carter,
Frederick R. Coudert, Professor Chandler, and Mrs.
Kinnicutt to demonstrate the probability that this
effort was " quiet, intelligent, and well-directed."
Nor, indeed, were the public officials unwilling to
co-operate with these citizens; on the contrary, the
universal testimony of them all was that both the
Tammany Mayor and the Tammany Board of Street
Cleaning showed the best possible disposition to do
the work they were put in office to do. Both this
distinguished group of citizens and the public officials with whom they were brought into contact
entertained the most cordial and earnest desire to
improve the condition of the streets. And yet what
was the result of this co-operation? Every man,
woman, or child who had to walk our streets during
the winter of 1892–'93 could testify but one way—
the result of this co-operation is admitted to have
been an unqualified failure. The fact is, that no
effort could succeed under the then existing system
of municipal government in securing the performance of the simplest and most obvious of its duties;
and the reason of this is so clear that it seems
hardly necessary to state it. Every office in this city,
from that of mayor to that of street-sweeper, was
either a reward for partisan service in the past or a

bribe for partisan service in the future. This does
not mean that the political organisation which distributed these offices was not desirous of governing
the city well; on the contrary, its maintenance in
power depended partly upon not outraging public
convenience too much. Tammany, therefore, was
keenly alive to the importance of keeping our streets
clean; but the relation of Tammany to its employees
was very much like that of the Roman Emperor to
the Prætorian guard—the servant was stronger than
the master. Those who occupied the public offices
did so because they controlled votes; these were
necessary to the maintenance of the political organisation which put and kept them in power, and for
this reason no effort, however earnest, however well-
directed, could with this material properly administer the business of the city. It was the political system which selected our public officials that alone
was responsible for the misgovernment to which we
so long submitted.

Again, the Association for Improving the Condition of the Poor has a department specially devoted
to the question of the sanitation of the houses of
the poor; it employs a number of inspectors who
have no other business than that of visiting tenement houses and reporting to the society such as are
in an unsanitary condition. The reports of these inspectors are submitted to the Board of Health for
action. Any one who desires to be informed regarding the working of this department can, by application to the secretary of the association, learn for

himself that every complaint made to the Health
Department is immediately attended to, provided
the owner of the house complained of has no " political pull "; but if the owner belongs to the machine which governs the city, no complaint, however
well-founded, receives adequate attention; and yet
no one will doubt the "quiet, intelligent, and well-
directed " character of the efforts of this Society for
Improving the Condition of the Poor.

In conclusion, if we need further illustration, let
us turn to the Health Department itself. To this
department is entrusted powers the magnitude of
which few citizens appreciate. Its officers can, without prior appeal to the courts, walk into any man's
house and turn him out of it upon an hour's notice.
It can close any factory, destroy any property, and
confine any individual, in case it deems such action
necessary to public health. These powers are granted to it in view of the public necessity that disease
should be immediately rooted out before it gets a
foothold, without regard to the individual inconven-
ience that it may occasion. Is it not, indeed, important that such powers as these be confided to men
whose position in the community offers some guarantee that they are not to be abused? No wonder
that our citizens were some time ago gratified to
learn that by the side of the department, possessing
as it does such autocratic power, there was placed an
advisory board of professional men occupying a high
position in the medical community, whose surveil-
lance furnished security that the acts of the Health

Board would be tempered by wisdom without losing
their executive force? And yet, what happened in
1892 in this department also? The superintend-
ent, who had for twenty-two years ably and satisfac-
torily performed his duties in connection with this
department, and had become an expert in the performance of these duties, was informed by the political organisation that then governed the city that his
place was needed for political purposes, and he was
required to send in his resignation upon an hour's
notice. The counsel to the board, who had satisfac-
torily occupied that position for about the same
period, and who had also acquired special and tech-
nical ability in handling the law work of this department, was practically dismissed in the same manner and for the same reason. The members of the
Advisory Board sent in their resignation one by one
in consequence of the injury done to the city by this
intrusion of partisanship into a department of our
city government which, clothed as it is with great
powers, should be least subject to partisan influence.
It was supposed that the citizens would be induced
by this courageous act of the Advisory Board to take
some action against the step which provoked it; but
the grip which Tammany had upon the city at the
time was too powerful, and the Health Board has
shared the fate of every other city department.

When we consider what questions the various
departments of the city have to deal with on the one
hand, and the character of the men to whom these
departments are entrusted on the other, we cannot

but recognise that, in the first place, the city is called
upon to handle and solve the greatest problems that
come up to us for solution, and that the solution of
these problems is left to men whom we know to be
neither able nor willing to undertake it. Not only
have they to keep our streets clean, our houses
wholesome, and our port free from infection, but
they have also to deal with such questions as pauperism, education, prostitution, and crime. Every one
of these problems is of incalculable difficulty, and
needs the application of all the result of human experience and the acumen of human sagacity. Most
of them need also reference to that religious sense to
which we are indebted for almost all the real advance that has been made on these subjects ; and
yet all the cities in the United States have, without
exception, practically to admit that these matters
have been abandoned to the hands of those who constitute the least competent class in the community,
and are themselves often the associates and partners
of crime.

But, as has been already repeatedly observed, this
condition of municipal government is one through
which we had to pass in order that the people might
learn from bitter experience that the universal franchise imposes a responsibility as well as confers a
benefit.

If we turn now from the actual evils attending
our municipal administration to the elements in the
community which give reasonable ground for hope
that these evils can be overcome, the prospect is an

11

encouraging one; for it is possible to demonstrate that not only is the majority of voters in favour of good government, but that whenever that majority has been appealed to in sufficiently rousing terms it has so declared itself. In 1893 an opportunity was given to test the people on this subject in the State of New York. The abuses which existed more or less in every election district in the State took a somewhat more aggravated form in that of Gravesend. The whole city of Brooklyn, too, had, since the last administration of Seth Low, taken a persistently downward path. These two considerations brought about an overturn in that city. A mayor was elected by a swingeing majority on the platform of good government; political offenders were subsequently landed in the penitentiary, and it may be said that in the fight between the people and the politicians the former came out entirely victorious. While this battle was waging in Brooklyn another battle of a similar character was fought in the State. A certain Isaac H. Maynard had been rewarded for juggling with election returns by an appointment to the Court of Appeals. His term of office having expired, the Democratic party, which was responsible for the appointment, and for bad government in the cities of Brooklyn and New York, nominated him for a new term. He was defeated by an overwhelming majority. These results are quite sufficient to satisfy us that the people who desire good government constitute a majority, and will so declare themselves if they are appealed to in sufficiently urgent terms to bring out the entire vote, and if the indignation aroused is sufficient to overcome partisan considerations. Nor can this be otherwise. It is inconceivable that a majority of citizens in any community can want bad government. The men who want bad government are those who prey upon the community. Because they commit their spoliations through our tolerance and under color of law we sometimes forget what they are ; but inasmuch as they elect themselves to office in spite of us and use their offices to blackmail and despoil us, we can hardly regard them in any other light than as freebooters. Now freebooters can never exist in greater numbers than those on whom they prey ; it is essential to a prosperous system of brigandage that the brigands be few and the victims many. This is the weak spot in all organisations for public plunder; when the organisation reaches its climax of success it must necessarily fall to pieces, for there is not then enough plunder to go around. Were the good citizens properly prepared, they could at such moments seize the succession. But they are seldom so prepared; they often sound the note of dissolution, but others collect the inheritance. Tammany has broken up more than once by the dissidence of malcontents, as when Irving Hall and Mozart Hall organised out of its *débris ;* and by the revolt of its respectable members, as when Abram S. Hewitt and others of his inclining founded the County Democracy. But Irving and Mozart Halls were never anything but rival machines, and the County Democracy soon got into the hands of men

as evil and less prudent than the leaders of Tammany. Nor was this matter for surprise. The bulk of
the men of New York, who work with limb and brain,
had not yet recognised the duty that popular government imposed on them ; they were not willing to devote the time necessary to preserve the County Democracy from the ever-present professional politician ;
and as Tammany was more on the alert for an occasion to destroy the County Democracy than the excellent citizens who organised it, the sinners in the
County Democracy were promptly landed in the penitentiary. And yet the melancholy fact must here be
chronicled, that amongst these men who carried the
colours of our last reform movement are some who
have been conspicuous for dishonesty amongst the
leaders of this defunct and discredited organisation.
This little piece of history has been told in order to
give a point to the following general conclusions :

In the first place, a corrupt machine must occasionally be defeated by its very success, for success
means increase in numbers, and increase in numbers
means more plunderers than plunder.

In the second place, such a breaking up, though
often brought about by disinterested men, does not
result in more than a momentary advantage, because
the citizens are not sufficiently organised to keep in
control.

In the third place, the spasmodic character of our
reform movements causes them often to be left in the
hands of new and inexperienced leaders, who are lack-
ing in the experience or the backbone necessary to

exclude from our ranks men whose past careers render them notoriously unfit allies to the cause. Society needs a remembrancer.

If, however, we recognised that ignorance was a crime ; if we kept ourselves so informed that forgetfulness was impossible ; if we devoted the necessary time to organisation—it is clear that we are in the majority, and that forces are continually at work on our side which must end in delivering over the enemy into our hands.

As matters now stand, however, it is clear from the foregoing considerations that our Government—and especially our municipal government—is not one by popular representation, but by popular misrepresentation. In other words, the elections, except under exceptional conditions, carry out the will not of the people, but of a few corrupt political leaders, and it is only rarely, fitfully, and under extraordinary circumstances that the real popular will is expressed. It is also clear that this is due to the fact that the citizen has abdicated in favour of political machines; that in so doing he has been guilty of a political crime; and that if he performed his clear political duty—that is to say, if he took the necessary steps to see that the proper candidates were nominated, and gave as much time to secure such nominations at periods of small excitement as he does at periods of great excitement—it would be perfectly possible, nay, easy, for him to have his way year in and year out. In other words, the citizen only attends to his political duties when driven to it by impulse and temper; he

never performs them for the same reason that he
does his domestic duties—because they *are* duties,
and he feels under a moral obligation to do so.   It
is believed that if the citizen knew what vital interests depended upon the yearly elections; if he were
alive to the uselessness of devoting his time to charitable and philanthropic societies so long as the administration of our public charities, of our public
schools, and of our public prisons was in the hands
of ignorant and self-seeking politicians; if he appreciated that it was idle to spend his money on private
charities so long as the money of the city was being
squandered in manufacturing the very paupers and
criminals which it was his aim to succour; if, in a
word, he understood that his well-intentioned efforts
have only for effect to trim the luxuriance of vice,
and by trimming to promote its growth, it is believed
that the energy, wealth, and disinterestedness that
now dissipate themselves in infructuous if not in
absolutely injurious effort would, by concentration
in better-directed channels, purge the State of politicians, relieve the labouring classes of the incubus of
pauperism, and largely diminish the effect of crime.
It is to this demonstration that the following chapters will be devoted.

CHAPTER X.

THE PROBLEM OF PAUPERISM.

Every city in the land is a gigantic mill daily engaged in withdrawing healthy labourers from the farm and converting them into paupers, lunatics, and convicts. We have taken the necessary course of constructing asylums for our lunatics, poorhouses for our paupers, and prisons for our criminals, but we have not attempted to deal with the failures in our population until they became so far demoralised as to be fit only for these dreary and expensive institutions. In fact, although the flow is always from the farm to the city, and never from the city to the farm, we have entirely failed to provide an outlet for the refuse of our population; on the contrary, we have provided a good cement bottom for it, so that none of our stagnant water can escape even if it would.

Of late, however, the study of sociology has begun to find and to apply new methods. The words of Seneca, "Pœna non irascitur sed cavet," are beginning to find an application in the substitution of reformatories for prisons, and in some countries the question of pauperism has also been handled by the

157

creation of what are known as labour colonies. It is questionable, however, if even in Holland the question of colonisation has reached anything more than the earliest stage. But in other parts of the world somewhat different experiments of a similar kind are being tried, and we are likely soon to have an accumulation of varied experience on the subject.

It has already been intimated that our present methods deal with the whole question too late. The fact is, the moment a man holds out his hand for alms he gives notice to society that he is caught in the outer edge of the whirlpool; private charity then keeps him alive only to increase his faculty for injuring the body politic. Except in cases of universal depression, where large quantities of worthy and willing labourers are unable to find employment on account of exceptional economic conditions, the man who asks for alms belongs to what may be called the " incapable " class. The word " incapable " is intended to include all persons who cannot work consecutively owing to temperamental defect, whether this defect be one of physique, of morale, of intelligence, or of temper, or whether it arise from illness, drunkenness, or any other cause beyond the pale of political economy. It will not do to wait until the incapable man has become a burden upon the parish after having become the father of a large family, or until he has qualified for jail after a career of crime; the process during which he gravitates towards the prison, the poorhouse, or the lunatic asylum is one fraught with as much evil for society as for himself.

It would be interesting to trace the evils for others to which this incapable man gives rise. Here are some of them :

1. He brings into the world children who are likely to become as incapable as himself. In addition to the well-known history of the " Jukes family," it may be interesting to note that researches lately made into the names of those enjoying public charity in France show that they tend from generation to generation to be the same—that is to say, those who generation after generation receive public benefaction belong to the same families.*

2. By being willing to accept alms he can content himself with a lower wage, thereby unfairly competing with the self-respecting labourer, and tending to drag down the rate below that necessary for sustenance. The working of outdoor relief in England has illustrated this.

3. He drains the pockets of his neighbours by appeals for help. No one who has investigated cases for the Charity Organization Society can fail to have discovered that poor people contribute large amounts to one another in times of distress. It is seldom that the pauper applies to the rich until he has exhausted the pockets of his neighbours.

4. He renders wholesome dwellings unwholesome by his shiftlessness and want of regard for sanitary rules. All those who have given much time to the question of sanitary tenements will testify to the

* Yves Guyot.

hopelessness of keeping tenements clean so long as there are shiftless tenants in the building. Whatever be the efforts made, and however great be the majority of tenants desirous of keeping their houses in good order, a single unclean tenant will be sufficient to make their efforts useless.

5. By failing to pay his rent and by perpetually moving from one tenement to another, he raises the rental for his fellow-tenants, the proprietor having to take account of "non-lets" in fixing his rent. An estimate of " non-lets " regularly enters into the determination of what rent must be charged in order to make a building pay. Every real estate agent is familiar with this fact.

6. By surrendering himself to laziness, drunkenness, and crime, he spreads the contagion of these vices to others.

The *laissez-faire* theory, that the pauper must not be treated but must be allowed to die, will not work. Experience shows that he does not die until he has done an incalculable amount of harm. Moreover, humanity and the proper extension of human sympathies make the application to man of the law of the survival of the fittest in this respect impossible. It is admitted that the criminal must be dealt with, but it does not seem to have been clearly understood that the incapable man is as hurtful to the community as the criminal. Moreover, our method of treating the criminal has not kept pace with our information. The simplest plan of educating chil-

THE PROBLEM OF PAUPERISM.

dren is to punish them whenever they annoy. This plan has yielded, in a civilised community, to more intelligent methods; children are punished less and less, and encouraged more and more. Persistent vice only is punished, and then for the purpose of treatment rather than for that of vindictiveness. No such progress has taken place in our penal legislation; we still pursue the old-fashioned plan of meting out punishment proportionately to the success of the criminal act. If, for example, a robbery be of a sum of money of less than twenty-five dollars, the criminal is punished by an imprisonment of not more than one year, or a fine of not more than five hundred dollars.* If a robbery be of a sum of over twenty-five dollars and under five hundred dollars, then the punishment is imprisonment for not less than two years nor more than five years. If a robbery be of a sum of more than five hundred dollars, then the punishment is not less than five years nor more than ten years. As if the amount that a thief succeeds in robbing has anything to do with the punishment he deserves, or the treatment that may be necessary in order to rescue society from further injury at his hands!

The moment we begin to consider the criminal as a human being to be reformed, and not as a sinner to be punished, there is no longer any reason for distinguishing, so far as the advisableness of treatment is concerned, between the criminal and the pauper;

* New York Penal Code, see sections 531, 532, 535, and 15.

both are dangerous; both are imperfectly responsible. The experience of the Elmira Reformatory shows that a large percentage of the criminal class can be reclaimed; it is probable that the same would be true of the pauper if we found the proper method of reclaiming him. The whole problem probably consists in selecting the best method.

Assuming that the Elmira Reformatory is pursuing a suitable line in the treatment of criminals and leaving the vexed subject of corporal punishment aside for the present, the question arises whether the same plan, or perhaps some more economical plan, might not be adopted with paupers; in other words, can previous efforts help us to devise a plan of colonisation that will effectually deal with the pauper as well as the criminal?

Much has been written and something done to prove the possibility of returning incapable men to the land, but schemes for doing this through the *voluntary* act of the incapable man must be at once eliminated (except in rare cases) as impracticable. It is the very nature of the incapable man to refrain from taking any step to improve his condition; he will not voluntarily subject himself to any discipline or labour. The success of the so-called labour colonies in Germany, which seem to be recruited by the voluntary action of paupers, has given rise to the notion in Europe that voluntary farm colonies would abolish tramps and poor-houses; this notion, however, is drawn from an imperfect knowledge of the working of the labour colony system in Germany. It is

true that labourers are not compelled by any decree
of a court to enter a labour colony or to remain there;
but they are practically forced into the labour colony
by the law of vagabondage which exists in Germany,
and they are compelled to remain there by the certainty that they must ultimately return if they leave
the colony without proper equipment for self-support. The system of *Natural-verpflegungs-stationen*,
taken in connection with section 361 of the German
penal code, practically leaves the tramp no recourse
but ultimately to shelter himself in a labour colony.
The above-mentioned section of the penal code permits a court to imprison tramps or persons falling
upon the parish, unless they can show that their poverty is due to circumstances for which they are not
responsible; but even then, the moment a man is
found begging he is at once put into one of the stations referred to, where he is given a night's lodging
and food, provided he does half a day's work; he is
given a certificate, called a *Wanderschein*, indicating
the place to which he is destined with a view to securing work, the route by which he is to go to this
place, and the stations where he is to be supplied
with food and lodging as in the first instance. As
each station is in communication with employers of
labour, it is practically certain that, except under un-
usual circumstances, a man who is willing to work
will eventually find it; consequently his failure to
find it raises a presumption of unwillingness or in-
capacity and secures his committal to the penitentiary. A pauper is thus put upon a track from which

he cannot escape, and which leads either to employment, to the penitentiary, or to a labour colony; in
other words, the labour colony is practically imposed
upon the incapable pauper as an alternative to the
penitentiary.

The development of this system in Germany is
due in great part to the licensed tramping which grew
out of the old rule, that skilled labourers should spend
two years in moving from town to town in search of
employment between the close of their apprentice-
ship and the day of starting out on their own account. That it is necessary to maintain such a net-
work of tramp stations as this in America or elsewhere, and thus encourage the tramp system, seems
extremely unlikely.

The purely penal colonies in Holland have demonstrated the fact that paupers and misdemeanants
can be supported upon land at about half the price
that they cost in the poor-houses in England,* and
that at the same time land can be reclaimed and
brought into cultivation under this system which it
would be too costly to reclaim by private enterprise.
In his work entitled Back to the Land, Mr. Moore
explains why these penal colonies are not self-supporting, and gives reasons for believing that, by somewhat changing the system, agricultural penal colonies could be made self-supporting. This is also the
opinion of the committee appointed to investigate
this matter on behalf of the English Land Colonisa-

---

* See Herbert V. Mills, Poverty and the State.

tion Society. The report of this last body, however, proposes to make the system self-supporting by devoting a very large area of land to the work. It is probable, however, that it proceeds upon somewhat wrong principles.

In the first place, the society proposes to create agricultural colonies, entrance to which and residence in which would be purely voluntary.

In the second place, it proposes that these colonies should be self-supporting by allowing four acres to a man.

Such a colony would undoubtedly be useful so long as there was a large proportion of worthy labourers unemployed. Experience, however, shows that this is seldom the case; that is to say, industrial crises giving rise to dismissal of worthy labourers are rare, and last relatively a short time. To organise a large permanent system of agricultural colonies to meet an evil which arises only once in ten or twenty years, is acute only for a few months and then disappears almost altogether, seems a mistake. The evil which is permanent does not arise from the unemployed who are willing to work; it arises from the unemployed who are unwilling to work, and whatever plan is suggested to meet the permanent evil must be one that deals with the unwilling.

The only alternative, therefore, seems to be a compulsory commitment of paupers to farm colonies conducted upon principles of military discipline, having grades of employment suited to the different classes of paupers, criminals, and unemployed with which it would deal, and in which criminals, unwilling and willing labourers, will all be carefully kept apart.

Such farm colonies need not necessarily be put upon a self-supporting basis. The reasons for not endeavouring to make them self-supporting are numerous.

In the first place, the class it would be destined to deal with now costs the State millions of dollars every year. These millions are devoted to keeping the evil alive. If they were devoted to quenching the evil they would be well spent, and the community could afford to pay them; but the very quenching of the evil would diminish the number to be treated, and so, without taking into account the economy of the proposal, the mere fact that the incapable man was being treated instead of being encouraged would diminish the expenditure. Nor is it the cost of the pauper which hurts the State so much as the injury which he inflicts upon the self-respecting workman with whom he competes, and whom, by competition and contact, he degrades.

In the second place, schemes of this character, which start on the expectation of being self-supporting and fail in being self-supporting, discourage those engaged therein.

In the third place, labour colonies, though not self-supporting, ought to be less expensive than existing methods. At present we have insane asylums of enormous cost, prisons of enormous cost, and workhouses of enormous cost, and in addition to these ten million dollars are known to be distributed annually by charitable societies in New York city alone, without including the millions annually spent by private individuals and private charities of which no record can be kept. The plan proposed ought greatly to diminish the cost of our existing institutions; it ought to bring into cultivation land not now cultivated; it ought to permanently improve land not now deemed capable of cultivation; and it ought, in a large measure, to diminish the necessity for private charity. With these advantages why attempt a self-supporting plan?

Another objection to the self-supporting plan is, that it involves the devoting to it of a larger quantity of land than perhaps can be conveniently spared. This objection, however, could be met by the adoption of a more suitable system of cultivation than the one usually employed by us. The Chinese plan, which proceeds upon the assumption that land is extremely valuable and human labor extremely cheap, is the one which will get the most out of the land in the way of subsistence for the largest number.

If the experiment of treating a large mass of paupers is to be tried, it is indispensable that the colony should not be at a great distance from the town. The product of their work requires a near market; expense of transportation, therefore, should be reduced to the minimum. Now it is near large towns that land is most valuable; hence the importance of adopting a system of agriculture which will support the largest number on the smallest surface.

12

As has been already suggested, this can best be achieved by the adoption of the Chinese system.

Agriculture is a part of the Chinese religion. The book of the Rise of the Dynasty of Tcheou contains an agricultural code, some of the most remarkable provisions of which are the following:

"The inspectors of agriculture should take care that the seed be properly prepared in manure. The grain must first be soaked in a bath of juice obtained by cooking beef bones; then, according as the seed is intended for land—that is, red, yellow, black or white, compact, friable or siliceous—they shall be soaked in fæcal matter (dried and reduced to a powder), whether of cattle, goats, sheep, swine, dogs, foxes, badgers, or deer."

In reference to human manure used by the Chinese the following extract provides:

"The inspectors of agriculture shall take care that no molecule of it shall be lost or wasted. It shall be collected in vases and shall ferment during six days. After this, use shall be made of it with ten times its bulk of water. For rice, it shall be poured over the ground during vegetation, not before, as much as is needed and no more; for it is not the land which must be nourished, but the plant; and if too much is poured over the land it evaporates in the air. As regards land not inundated, it shall be deposited at the foot of the plants while growing; for if it were put between the lines a large part would be lost. By so acting with wisdom and economy little will be spent, an abundant harvest will be reaped, and the people will be prosperous. In the north provinces, which do not produce a harvest during the winter, the manure not used shall be mixed up with the earth and made into bricks, which shall be transported to the south provinces."

Two other special features of Chinese agriculture must not be overlooked, namely, the use of water and transplanting.

Much labour has been usefully expended in constructing irrigation canals, by which water is distributed over the entire country. Undoubtedly a large part of the fertility of the soil is due to these important works. In no way could pauper or convict labour be used to better advantage.

But it is in their use of frequent transplanting that Chinese methods perhaps differ mostly from ours. All the crops are practically treated in China in the same way as spring vegetables are treated by us ; that is to say, all seed is planted in rich mould, under glass if necessary, or, if not, under glass protected by a wall from the north winds, and with a southern exposure. After the seed has sprouted the plant is transplanted, sometimes once, sometimes twice, and sometimes even thrice. The advantages arising from this system are manifold. In the first place, all the time during which the seed is germinating it is occupying a very small surface, and the land where it is destined ultimately to bring fruit is being employed in another crop. In this way the same field is made to bear many crops in the same season.

In the second place, the plant is made more

vigorous by transplanting. The descending root is replaced by a multitude of horizontal roots, which give the plant strength and serve to pick up nourishment from the surface, thereby making deep digging unnecessary. A single grain of wheat cultivated in this manner has multiplied itself as many as sixty times. Luzerne has been harvested twelve to fourteen times instead of once.

In the third place, there is an economy of seed. For a single acre a few pints of grain are sufficient, instead of the usual bushels.

In the fourth place, there is an economy of labour in the area which is to be cultivated in order to produce this result.

Plants which are grown in this way by us tend to be weak; this is counterbalanced by the system of soaking in manure already referred to.

Another advantage derived from this kind of culture is, that it permits of the introduction of annual plants borrowed from warmer climates. Thus in Mongolia the winters are long and cold, the temperature descending to thirty degrees below zero; the summers, though warm, are short—so short, indeed, that potatoes freeze in the middle of September. Under ordinary culture nothing but grass could live; by transplanting, however, wheat ripens at the end of August. The herbaceous cotton-plant is also acclimated by the same method.

Another advantage resulting from this system is, that the ravages of hail and inundations are immediately repaired, by the fact that there is always in reserve a large quantity of plants ready to be transplanted at any time. Though hail may destroy a particular crop, there is always another crop ready to substitute therefor.

What this culture can do may be judged from the number of inhabitants which any one given district supports. For example, the district of Ouang Mokhi, described by Simon, contains twelve hundred hectares, or say three thousand acres, and supports ten thousand inhabitants—that is to say, three to an acre. Contrast this with the four acres to a man proposed by the English Land Colonisation Society. One of the subsidiary advantages of this garden culture is that it relieves the country from its dreariness. Such a population as this has all the advantages of a town, with none of its disadvantages; for every district has numerous pagodas or communal buildings, which, though used mainly for religious purposes, serve also for markets, clubs, and theatrical performances.

The Chinese peasant does not confine himself to agriculture; he carefully provides himself with raw material for occupation during those hours which he cannot spend in the field. For example, he makes his own linen, cotton, silk, and therefore his own clothes; he makes his own oil; and though these articles are not made as cheaply by hand as by factory labour, yet he produces so much more of the raw material to the acre that the net result is an advantage to him. Take, for example, the oil that is derived from the turnip seed: whereas our factories

would get thirty-three kilos of oil from one hundred
kilogrammes of seed, the Chinaman only gets twenty-
five and twenty-eight. But one hectare produces for
them twenty-two hundred and fifty kilogrammes
of grain, whereas for us only fourteen to fifteen hundred; the advantage, therefore, is on his side by one
hundred kilos of oil more than for us. The same result can be worked out for sugar.

Culture of this kind is by no means deadening
to the intelligence; on the contrary, the Chinese
peasant is intensely wide-awake; the necessity of
adapting his methods to his climate, the changing
conditions of the seasons, and the fact that he con-
trives to provide himself with industrial occupations
when not engaged in the field, make of him a very
different human being from the agricultural labourer
as he is known in England.

No effort, however, to deal with the incapable is
likely to prove successful unless he is exposed to the
process of military discipline. The notion that the
pauper cannot be made to work is due, I think, to
an entire misconception as to the methods which
might be adopted to make him work. As has been
already stated, no labour colony organised upon the
voluntary system will ever achieve much with the
incapable; and as long as philanthropists have in
their minds the possibility of *persuading* the pauper
to work on land, all efforts in the compulsory direction are likely to be kept waiting. They do not seem
to have considered the notion of applying military

discipline to these men. What military discipline can do for them is evidenced by what it does for the army, which is recruited, in England at least, from the very dregs of the population. The public tolerates flogging for insubordination in the army, because it has been handed down by tradition as right and proper; but if it is necessary to flog in order to make good soldiers and sailors, why should we shrink from adopting the same method for rescuing unwilling paupers from misery and crime? But a very little consideration will suffice to show that practically no flogging would be necessary. Recourse is now seldom had to it in the army or navy. Two regulations have in England lately contributed to reduce the amount of flogging almost to zero, viz. First, that flogging must never be imposed on the same day that the offence is committed; second, that every case of flogging must be reported at headquarters. If such conditions were imposed at the Elmira Reformatory there probably would never have been occasion for the distressing differences which have lately harassed the public mind regarding this admirable institution. But it will never be necessary to apply corporal punishment in pauper colonies. If different colonies were started for the three different classes of persons above referred to—viz., the criminal, the incapable, and the willing unemployed—a system of transfer from one to the other would furnish a method of punishment in one direction and of advancement in the other. Mistakes are certain to be made in commitments to these various colonies. To the colonies for the willing unemployed many incapables are likely to find their way; these will have to be sifted out, so that they may be subjected to the more rigorous discipline of the colony for incapables, and so as not to contaminate the willing workers to which these colonies should be confined. Again, when an inmate of the colony for incapables becomes refractory he ought to be transferred to the criminal colony, the discipline of which would be still more rigorous. Under this system corporal punishment need only be applied, if at all, in the criminal colony. On the other hand, when a member of the criminal colony deserved advancement he could be transferred to the incapable colony; from that again to the colony of the willing unemployed; and so, eventually, when he has earned the right to it, to freedom.

One last necessary provision in our new legislation on this subject should not be omitted. After all efforts to reform have proved vain, the refractory subject should be confined for life under conditions too unhappy to fail to act as a strong deterrent. If society owes shelter and food to those who will not work, it owes them nothing but the barest shelter and the least expensive food—military discipline, a board bed, bread and water, and no more. Nothing would deter more than the certainty that this awaited the refractory incapable.

The above considerations seem to point to the following conclusions:

The indeterminate sentence should be substituted for the fixed term.

The methods now adopted at the Elmira Reformatory should be extended to penal farm colonies, which should be kept strictly apart from pauper farm colonies.

There should be two classes of pauper farm colonies, viz.: First, those to which magistrates should be authorised to commit all persons asking alms, male or female, all drunken or disorderly persons, and all persons convicted of habitual drunkenness; second, those to which are destined all paupers willing to work. These two classes of colonies—which may be called respectively unwilling pauper colonies and willing pauper colonies—should be kept strictly apart.

In penal colonies and unwilling pauper colonies the sexes should be separated, so as to prevent increase of population during the period of commitment.

There should be a system of graduation provided from the penal to the unwilling pauper colonies, and from the unwilling pauper colony to the willing pauper colony.

Willing pauper colonists, when found capable of self-support, should be provided with farms in the West, a purchase-money mortgage being taken for cost of farm, buildings, stock, and equipment. Then and then only, should families that have been separated by commitment be reconstituted.

Military discipline should prevail in both the

penal colony and the unwilling pauper colony, but corporal punishment should be tolerated, if at all, only in the purely penal colonies.

Every colony should be constituted with the view of making it as self-supporting as possible. To this end every colony should give occupation to all the trades necessary to a complete colony, thus profiting to the utmost by all skilled labour therein, and furnishing to the unskilled and to children the opportunity of acquiring a trade. It would be perfectly possible so to control this part of the colonisation scheme that the work of these skilled labourers should never compete with labour outside the colony; in other words, so much time only should be given to this work as would provide the colonies with the articles of each trade which they can use respectively. The time not required in the trade should be employed on the farm. Moreover, there could be an exchange of products between the colonies and the penal institutions of the State that would greatly diminish any difficulty arising from this source.

All the willing pauper colonies ought to be near the city, on fertile ground, and devoted mainly to the production of vegetables for the city market under the Chinese system. Proximity is important in view of the character of the product, and the fact that the population of these colonies would be in part transient, and the expense of transporting paupers from the city to such a colony and back to the city ought to be rendered as small as possible.

The unwilling pauper colonies might, on the other hand, be further removed from the city, all their inmates being necessarily committed for a term of some length. They might be employed upon poorer land and in the production of larger crops.

Penal colonies could be still further removed from the city and put to the less grateful work of reclaiming bad land, more attention being paid to the methods used than to the results obtained.

A system of profit-sharing might be introduced in the willing pauper colony.

It is not claimed that the adoption of this plan is sure to deal successfully with the problem involved. The success of it will depend upon the administration of the colonies. But if some of those who are now spending days and nights in struggling with the insoluble problem of pauperism within the city will turn their attention, their zeal, and their intelligence to the administration of pauper colonies outside the city, and if, by the success of these colonies, our streets and tenement houses be rid of the drunkard, the unclean, the thriftless, the quasi-criminal, and the criminal himself, it is believed that a long step will have been taken towards relieving the misery which the presence of this class in our cities causes to the working man.

The foregoing suggestions are made without attempting to discuss whether pauperism can be attacked in its source—viz., wasteful production and unequal distribution of commodities. This last

question, which will be treated in the chapter on
Socialism, is one which we must reconcile ourselves
to postpone. Even if we conclude that the socialist
programme is one that can to any extent be carried
out, it is perfectly clear that it cannot be carried out
for many years, if not centuries. The glaring defects, however, in our method of dealing with pauperism and crime are productive of too immediate
evil not to demand urgent attention, especially in
view of the fact that the remedy for the evil set
forth in the preceding pages is one that could be
applied without delay.

But it would be useless to attempt the plan suggested unless it were possible to find men and women
having the capacity, moral as well as intellectual, to
carry it out in the spirit in which it is suggested.
Any attempt to carry it out through the instrumentality of officers elected or appointed under the
conditions which prevail in our municipalities to-day
must be doomed to failure.* The treatment of the
incapable is one of extreme difficulty. Not only
does it involve insight into character and consum-
mate judgment, but, what is more important, an
unruffled temper. Such qualities as these are not
likely to be found united in appointees of our present political machines. So long, therefore, as these
are in control of our municipal offices it is hopeless
to endeavour to put such a plan in execution.

How hopeless it is to think of getting good ad-

* Written before November 6, 1894.

ministration under our present political system may
be seen from an examination of the way in which
paupers and criminals are treated in any one of our
large cities. With the single exception of the Fire
Department, which, though honeycombed with small
abuses, is nevertheless efficient for the purpose for
which it was organised, probably the best administered department in the city of New York is that of
Charities and Correction. The law under which
this department is organised is conceived in a large
and philanthropic spirit.* Much is left—as it should
be—to the discretion of the commissioners. They
are given full and exclusive powers for the management, maintenance, and direction of all the prisons,
penitentiaries, hospitals, almshouses, workhouses,
nurseries, and lunatic asylums in the city. It is provided that there should be two bureaus—one of
charities and one of correction. The bureau of correction should have charge of all matters relating to
criminals; that of charities should have charge of all
matters relating to persons not criminals. The commissioners are authorised to maintain an industrial
school at Hart's Island, but this is left to the commissioners. They are also authorised to maintain an
asylum for inebriates, but this also is left to the commissioners. Large discretion is also given to them
as regards transfers from the city prison, penitentiary, or almshouse, to the workhouse, and as regards
the employment of all persons whose age or health

---

* Consolidation Act, chap. x.

permits of their working. They are authorised to
punish any convict or pauper who refuses to perform
the work allotted to him by feeding him on bread
and water only, and may "open an account with all
paupers committed to the workhouse, charging them
with the expenses incurred by the city for their
board, and crediting them with a reasonable compensation for the labour performed by them, so that
at the expiration of the term of sentence any balance
found due them shall be paid to them in cash."
They are required to keep paupers and criminals
separated, and so to classify the criminals that the
" novices in crime may not be contaminated by the
evil example or by association or contact with the
more hardened or confirmed." They are required
to give employment to children in the nurseries, and
authorised to bind out children as apprentices. Last,
but not least, no criminal or vagrant can be discharged without their approval.

In the course of the investigation of the administration of the city departments by the Senate Committee, under resolution adopted January 20, 1890,
the President of the Board of Charities and Correction was examined.[*] The department had not given
rise to any special cause of complaint. The president of the board was considered to have been a
good appointment, made by a good mayor, at a time
when the city had been temporarily rescued from
Tammany Hall. Under these circumstances, there-

---

* Report, vol. iv, pp. 3326-3451.

fore, the management of the department was likely
to give rise to the least criticism, and yet these are
some of the admissions that the president was obliged
to make :

The law requires the commissioners to create two
distinct bureaus, one of charities and one of correction, for the express purpose of preventing the possibility of contact between paupers and criminals.
Nor was this left to the discretion of the commissioners; upon this point the law was mandatory.
Nevertheless, the president was obliged reluctantly
to admit that there had been persistent failure to
comply with the law in this respect.* Moreover, no
attempt had been made to classify criminals, so that
" novices in crime might not be contaminated by association with the more hardened or confirmed "; †
on the contrary, from motives of economy, women of
bad character were distributed for work among the
hospital and other institutions,‡ and inmates of the
asylum were often assigned to the same work as
those of the penitentiary.# Whenever the commissioners might have exercised their discretion in a hu-
manitarian sense they had failed to do so. There was
no industrial school at Hart's Island;‖ there was no
asylum for inebriates;△ no account had ever been
opened with paupers with a view to furnishing them
with a fund at the expiration of their term; ◊ there

---

* Id., p. 3327.   # P. 3342.   ◊ P. 3381.
† P. 3335.   ‖ Pp. 3364, 3367.
‡ P. 3344.   △ P. 3369.

were no nurseries ; * and no children had ever been
bound out as apprentices.† It was admitted that the
accommodations were grossly defective, though it was
explained that this was due to the refusal of the financial board of the city to furnish the necessary funds
for increasing the buildings proportionately to the
increase of occupants.‡ The president admitted
that all the commissioners and employees owed their
appointments—or, in the case of the president himself, his maintenance in office—to political influence ; #
and, although all applicants for employment were
obliged to pass a civil-service examination, "a Democrat would be very apt to get there." Needless to
say, Mr. Porter, the president, was a Democrat. It
was also admitted that the discharges in the month
of October—that is to say, the month immediately
preceding elections—were one hundred per cent
more than in any other month of the year. The
examination here is worth quoting at length :

"Now, I find, by going over such statistics as I
have, that the discharges usually are a hundred per
cent more in the month of October than they are in
any month of the year."

"I guess you and I understand that."

"We understand it, but I want the committee
to understand it. Why is it, Mr. Porter ?"

"Well, I don't know. They discharge them."

---

* Id., p. 3382.   † P. 3385.   ‡ P. 3406.

P. 3400: "Well, I suppose we all do more or less get our
appointment through political influence."

" Police justices discharge them ? "

" Yes, sir."

" And you do not exercise your prerogative of withholding your counter-signature ? "

" No."

Perhaps the defect of a system which puts the administration of city departments into the hands of politicians is best illustrated by the explanation given for the failure to institute an industrial school at Hart's Island. Mr. Porter testified that it was impossible to run an industrial school, " because you no more than get a boy fairly started than his discharge comes. . . . But if the terms were settled, if a boy who was noted for being a disorderly boy in his district were committed to the workhouse and was intended to stay there for his term and then to be sent to an industrial school, why, something might be accomplished ; but so long as they are to be discharged, some of them a few days after their committal, why, the school can effect but little."

Mr. Porter entirely forgot, when he so testified, that no inmate of this institution could be discharged without his consent and that of the commissioners. All, therefore, that he had to do was to refuse his consent, and thus prevent the discharge of a boy who had not been long enough in the industrial school to reap advantage therefrom. But when Mr. Porter was asked whether he ever exercised his right to refuse his consent, he testified that he did not.*

* Id., p. 3351.

13

"Have you ever refused to make a discharge where a police justice has signed the discharge?"

"No, I do not think I ever have, sir."

In other words, this power of discharge is a power exercised by police justices for the purpose of securing a political following among the criminal classes and for the purpose of securing votes prior to election. Mr. Porter would be injuring the opportunities for patronage of his fellow-politicians if he refused to consent to a discharge, although under the law he has a right to do so. It is politics, therefore, that prevents the commissioners from doing their duty.

How little they are alive to the evils which they are supposed to handle in their department may also be judged from a toleration of the system by which habitual offenders, or "old rounders" as they are called,* are regularly committed for drunkenness and disorderly conduct only to be discharged again, and then recommitted and redischarged. Mr. Porter testifies that, in his opinion, they ought to be obliged to serve the whole term of six months; but in this case also he does not exercise the discretion allowed him by which he can refuse to consent to their discharge at a prior date. And so the workhouse is practically converted into a boarding house for drunkards; it can hardly be considered a place of confinement. They are regularly set at liberty, and remain at liberty long enough for a debauch, and

* Id., p. 3350.

are willingly enough committed after the debauch is over during the time necessary for making them fit and disposed for another. Mr. Porter is perfectly alive to the evil, and has apparently not lifted a finger to suppress it.

It has been already stated that the financial authorities in the city, called the Board of Estimate and Apportionment, do not provide the funds necessary for the working of the Department of Charities and Correction. The estimates made by the department are regularly and arbitrarily cut down by the board, and applications for funds necessary for additional buildings are refused. The reason of this is not far to seek; in the language of ward politics, there is no money in this department for Tammany Hall. The voluntary organisation known as the State Charities Aid Association has secured the right of visiting all the public institutions of an eleemosynary nature in the State, and the vigilance of this society makes it difficult for Tammany to make anything out of this department. But nothing, perhaps, serves better to demonstrate the hopelessness of the effort to get good work out of public officials under a Tammany *régime* than the effect of this aid society upon our charitable institutions. It has undoubtedly accomplished a great work, and is entitled to the gratitude of every citizen who has the interests of the poor and wretched at heart; but because of the very good it does, because of the very vigilance it exercises, Tammany can make nothing out of the department, and Tammany therefore cuts down the appropriations which otherwise would be lavished upon it. But it is not by peculation only that Tammany ruins our public service, for President Porter testified that he did not do his duty in refusing discharges made for political purposes, and that he owed his position to political influences. It does not require much sagacity to make the connection.

So long as political machines control our city offices, no efforts of the State Charities Aid Association, or the Charity Organisation Society, or the Society for Improving the Condition of the Poor, or the hundreds of other societies in the city, will do more than dam the evils that flow from municipal misgovernment.

The present administration of our municipal charities in New York is the very best that can be expected from such administration of municipal affairs as we now have; it is a matter for congratulation that it is not infinitely worse. And yet it does not pretend to make an effort to deal with the real problems of pauperism. The commissioners seem to do the least possible in the performance of their duties. There is no idea of improving the condition of the men in these institutions, or otherwise grappling with the distressing questions to which the treatment of the pauper and criminal gives rise. The contrast shown in the preceding pages between what ought to be done for the criminal, the pauper, and the incapable, and what is done for them, taken in connection with the political conditions under which all our municipal departments are adminis-

tered, ought to bring it home to the mind of every
earnest man that he cannot better employ the time
that he has to give to charitable work than in the
correction of the *political system* which puts into
office men who, however willing, are, in consequence
of the political conditions by which they are surrounded, incapable of executing the law.

It is a matter of record that over ten million dollars are annually spent in charity in the city of New
York. This, of course, does not include the millions
which are spent by individuals, of which no record
is kept. The Board of Estimate and Apportionment,
to whom is confided the distribution of the funds of
the city amongst the various departments, have year
after year refused to appropriate the sum of less than
a million asked for the completion of necessary buildings, and the whole appropriation made for the support of our prisoners, paupers, sick, and insane is
about two million dollars a year. If the sums which
are now willingly contributed by societies to the relief of distress in this city were added to that appor-
tioned by the city for the same purpose, and both
were intelligently applied to the treatment of this
class, it is believed that, in the first place, more than
half the fund would be found to be superfluous; that,
in the second place, pauperism would, *in so far as it
tends to degrade the workingman*, practically disappear from the streets of the city; and, in the third
place, a merciful but implacable severity to those
who refuse to work would prevent all danger of at-
tracting paupers from outside.

CHAPTER XI.

PROBLEM OF SOCIALISM.

It has been pointed out in the preceding chapter that the workingman is materially injured by our neglect to intelligently handle the question of pauperism and crime. He is injured by the return to the community of the criminal after imprisonment, without any guarantee that the criminal has been reformed, but rather with the certitude that in consequence of the stigma of imprisonment he is committed to a career of crime. He is injured by the regular return to his neighbourhood of the "rounder," whose release affords opportunity for renewing the offences which regularly return him to the workhouse. He is injured by the incapable man, who lowers wages by his willingness to accept alms; who drains the pockets of his neighbours by appeals to their charity; who renders wholesome dwellings unwholesome by his uncleanliness; who increases the rental to his fellow-tenants by failing to pay rent himself, and who spreads contagion about him—the contagion of laziness, drunkenness, and vice.

The workingman is more heavily handicapped in this matter than he himself at all appreciates. It

is not likely, however, that he would recognise efforts
made to handle this problem as in any way a benefit
to himself; his mind is too resolutely turned in an
opposite direction; he has learned to expect and believe in a more radical cure; he has been taught by
Carl Marx that the conflict between labour and capital
is ineradicable; he has been tortured by unsuccess-
ful strikes into hating his employer, and exhilarated
by successful strikes into despising him; he has acquired just enough knowledge of political economy
to appreciate the injustice of his position as compared with that of the idle rich, and he is firmly
convinced of the possibility of securing justice by
the destruction of private property, and the vest-
ing of the title to both land and commodities in the
State. The demand of the People's party for the
ownership by the Government of railroads, telegraphs, and telephones; the declaration that land is
the heritage of the people; the demand for free and
unlimited coinage of silver at the ratio of sixteen to
one; of the increase of circulating medium to fifty
dollars *per capita;* of graduated income tax; and of
a system of loaning money to the farmers, known as
the sub-treasury plan, at two per cent. per annum,
and the fact that this party polled over a million
votes in 1893, and actually carried Colorado, Idaho,
Kansas, Nevada, and North Dakota, indicate that
this belief in socialistic measures not only widely
prevails but is becoming organised.

The demands of the Socialist Labour party are
still more extensive; they include the right of initia-

tive and referendum in the people, the abolition of
the presidency, the vice-presidency, and Senate of
the United States, and a large number of other constitutional changes of a radical character. This party
polled nearly eighteen thousand in New York, which,
if added to sixteen thousand five hundred polled by
the Populists, make a total vote of thirty-four thousand in favour of Socialist measures in this State.

The political attitude of the workingman in
New York city is still more deserving of our consideration than appears from these figures; for in municipal matters he unhesitatingly states that he will
continue to support Tammany Hall irrespective of
its dishonesty and corruption, because it is the estab-
lished policy of Tammany Hall to favour large public
works, and because in the execution of these public
works high rates of wages are paid to the labourer and
union labourers are preferred. For example, a street
sweeper receives two dollars a day from the city,
whereas if the work were done by contract he would
receive from a contractor not more than one dollar a
day. When it is pointed out to the wage earner that
it is folly to increase the scope of the Government as
long as the Government is in such bad hands, he
answers that it is the wealthy who pay for Tammany's dishonesty—not the poor. The matter is to
these last not one of more or less taxation; it is one
of life and death.

And this is not an over-statement. During the
winter of 1893–'94, had it not been for the vigorous
efforts of the private charities, thousands would have

perished of starvation in the street. That the imminence of such a danger should have left a profound impression on the minds and hearts of the labouring man is hardly a matter for surprise.

It may be claimed that the argument of hunger is not a permanent one, but resulted from the exceptional industrial conditions which prevailed during that winter, and are not likely soon to prevail again. Though this is undoubtedly true to a certain extent, there are permanent forces at work tending towards socialism which we cannot fail to recognise. It is universally admitted that the industrial revolution which resulted from the inventions of the latter part of the last century, by removing labourers from their homes, where they supported themselves by individual work, and collecting them in large factories where they earn their living by collective work, naturally directed the minds of the working people towards the possibility and simplicity of a social system which should replace the capitalist by the State. Under the old dispensation they owned their tools themselves; under the new dispensation these tools had become transformed by mechanical inventions into huge and expensive machinery, and had become the property of factory owners. This machinery could only be purchased by large capitalists, who are thus put in a position to dictate terms to the workman, and to put him under rules and regulations that fall little short of military discipline. The very fact that large industries had, before their very eyes and in their own experience, become monopolised in a

few factories owned by private capital, naturally suggested to the minds of the workmen a more complete monopoly in the hands of the State, the profits
of which should be returned to the wage earner,
who seemed the most entitled to them.

Again, while the tendency of industrial evolution to-day is towards the massing of workingmen
in large factory towns, and the creation of practical
monopolies which seem to prepare them for expro-
priation by the State, one important conservative
force in the community which would tend to resist
this movement towards socialism, is being daily weakened. The family, which is the basis of our civilisation, is gradually breaking up. Marriage, which
religion originally rendered indissoluble, has now,
by the breaking down of religion, by the laxity of
divorce legislation, and by the disappearance of the
public condemnation of divorce, become too often a
time contract. With the relaxation of the marriage
tie comes naturally a disintegration of the family
institution, of which marriage was, in the age of
faith, an indissoluble cement. And not only is the
family tending to break up and the marriage tie to
become weakened, but factory work is tending more
and more to separate men from women. Thus, some
manufacturing towns in New England are popular-
ly called "she-towns," because they consist mainly
of women and children, whereas the men drift away
to logging camps, mining camps, and the boarding
tents of the iron region. In Paul Gohre's work
entitled Three Months a Factory Hand he describes

the tendency of the family to disappear and to be replaced by boarding-houses, in which kinship becomes subsidiary to convenience of locality. The moral effect of such a system is considerable. The children practically escape entirely from the control of their parents, who become to them nothing more than fellow-boarders. The feeling of responsibility which the head of a family entertains for the support of his wife and children tends to disappear, and with it the spirit of conservatism that generally ranks itself in favour of maintaining existing institutions.

Education, too, especially in the homœopathic doses furnished to the working class, is creating a spirit of discontent amongst the working people which is likely eventually to express itself in a demand for revolutionary changes. It is inconceivable that the labouring man can slowly increase in knowledge without at the same time increasing in the faculty which springs from knowledge. His patience in bygone days resulted mainly from mental inactivity. The moment his brain becomes stimulated by education and a weapon is put into his hands by knowledge, there can be but one result— he will demand that his position be bettered.

Nor is there any reason to expect that the demands of a workman for improvement of his condition would be wise or moderate. The education he receives is sufficient to discontent, but not sufficient to instruct him. He often fails to distinguish between the injustice of a greedy capitalist and the exigencies of a particular industrial condition. He

often strikes when he should not, and sometimes re-
frains from striking when he should. Moreover,
every strike, whether it succeeds or fails, tends to
widen the breach between himself and his employer.
Nothing tends more to create revolutionary changes
than the opposition of two classes who are, or who
believe themselves to be, irremediably antagonistic.
It is when two electrically charged bodies are separated by a nonconducting material, across which
opposing electricities can with difficulty travel, that
the accumulation becomes dangerous. Make the
material between them a better conductor, and what
would otherwise have been an explosion will become
an interchange. The upper middle class, which
serves as a continual hyphen between the aristocracy
and the lower middle class in England, has prevented the revolution which took place in France,
owing to the absence of this very class. So, let the
tension between the employer and the employee continue to increase as it has increased in the past, and
nothing but a revolution can clear the air. But let
there step in between these warring elements a body
of their fellow-citizens willing to undertake a careful, earnest, and intelligent consideration of the
problems which now divide them, and it is confidently believed that danger of revolutionary measures can be avoided.

And we cannot afford to disregard the dangers
of such a revolution. The workingman is creating
a wide sympathy in the community; he is becoming
organised, educated, and strong, and he is also be-

coming conscious of his strength. Under these conditions his demands are likely to be put forward in such a form as, by striking down capital, to destroy the very basis upon which all civilisation is founded; whereas, if these demands are propounded with moderation and in such a form as to transfer the capital without destroying it, all danger arising from socialistic demands will disappear, and out of a gradual trial of socialistic measures which may result in the permanent adoption of some and the permanent rejection of others, the community will emerge strengthened and improved.

It must not be supposed that socialism is necessarily revolutionary. Upon no subject is there more widespread ignorance as well as indifference than socialism. Many would be astounded to learn that socialism and anarchism are absolutely opposed to one another. They would be surprised to learn that socialism involves no sudden transference of property from the individual to the State. The majority of the County Council in London are practically socialists. The same is true of the Municipal Council in Paris and the principal towns of France, and the Social Democrats are to-day numerically the strongest party in the German Empire. The London County Council is now actually engaged in carrying out a socialist programme, and this without the slightest dislocation or interruption of continuous municipal administration.

Socialism is no more capable of definition than religion, for, like religion, it is an outgrowth of

conditions which, though they have some features
in common all over the world, differ materially in
other respects in different countries. Just as the
God of the Greek has been already pointed out to
have differed from the God of the Hebrew, in much
the same manner as the needs of the Greek temperament differed from those of the Hebrew temperament, so the socialism of Germany differs from
the socialism of England in much the same manner
as the needs of the German differ from the needs of
the English workingman. To the German the State
is "an organised power for the maintenance of the
actually existing social relations of property and
class domination." An empire which grew out of a
successful war under the tutelage of Von Moltke
and Bismarck, and is now delivered over by heredi-
tary accident to a young man who unites in himself
the autocratic temperament of both; arbitrary, bu-
reaucratic, and military in its essential character-
istics; putting its concessions to socialism in the
most offensive possible form, and then thrusting
them down the throats of the people, as it were,
with a sword, is not the form of government likely
to endear itself to the German socialist. This last
declines any longer to be treated as a child, for he
believes himself to understand his needs as well as
the young gentleman who now occupies the Prussian
throne. Two facts peculiar to Germany, therefore,
tend to stamp German socialism with peculiar char-
acteristics. In the first place, Germany is a country
in which compulsory education has been longest in

force. German socialism is therefore more highly educated than the socialism of any other country; and not only is it more highly educated, but, in accordance with the temperament of German thought, tends to be philosophical and abstract in its terms. In the second place, the Government being in the hands of a military aristocracy, it is hated by the socialist, who, though he wants education and insurance, does not want either on the condition of its being compulsorily administered by the State. Hence the German is opposed to those measures which, inasmuch as they are imposed by an aristocratic State, have acquired the name of State socialism.

In England, on the other hand, totally different conditions prevail. Compulsory education is comparatively recent. The people are practical rather than philosophical, and the State, though still haunted with ghosts of the *ancien régime*, is practically democratic. In other words, what socialist measures have been adopted, instead of being compulsorily imposed by a government essentially hostile to the workingman, are, as a matter of fact, administered by a democratic government of which the workingman forms a part and as regards the working of which he has a voice. For this reason socialists in England tend to be practical, and are in favour of the very State socialism so obnoxious to socialists in Germany.

After this preamble regarding the points on which socialism is likely to differ under different conditions, let us now consider those points in which it tends to be the same.

Socialism is practically an effort to solve the problem of economical production and just distribution. It is clear that under existing conditions the goods of this world are not only unevenly but unjustly distributed. Moreover, they are not only unevenly but wastefully produced. Wastefulness of production under the competitive system is illustrated by the paralleling of railway lines and the duplication of gas and telegraph companies, creating momentary competition which eventually only tends to swell a monopoly at enormous unnecessary cost. It is further illustrated by the waste and expense of advertising and commercial travelling, which are both purely the product—and often the mendacious product—of competition; by the inability of the producer to know beforehand in what quantities various commodities are to be produced; by the inevitable waste consequent upon over-production of one article and under-production of others, hindsight being thus deliberately substituted for foresight in a matter concerning which foresight would seem to be indispensable. This condition of things results in industrial crises, the losses attending which are incalculable; capital remains idle, labour unemployed, the production of work ceases, and want, starvation, and vice follow as necessary consequences. If production were in the hands of the State these difficulties would be eliminated. Railroads would be built where they were needed, and only where they were needed. The same would be true of gas mains and telegraph wires. The amount of commodities needed would be known, and labour would be transferred from the production of one kind to another without the necessity of calamitous crises to compel the transfer.

The problem of distribution is a more difficult one. A system which gives a few men more millions a year than they can spend and keeps a tenth part of our population in misery and want cannot be wise or just. It is this glaring inequality in the distribution of products which commends the study of socialism most to the workingman, and ought to commend it most to the man of morality and justice. On the other hand, it is the waste of production in our existing system which commends it most to the economist.

It would be a profound mistake to suppose that, because the platforms of various socialist bodies are radical and even revolutionary, no measures propounded by socialists are worthy of consideration. How much there is in the socialist programme which deserves study, if not adoption, at our hands may be gathered by a brief statement of what is termed the London Programme of the Fabian Society.

The demands of the Fabian programme are eight in all :

1. The unearned increment: By this expression is meant the amount added to the selling value of land by the mere increase in the size of the community and in its productive power. In other words, it is the increase in the value of land through the

14

industry and intelligence of the working population, which piles up millions of increased value for the few who own the land, and who, if idle, contribute nothing thereto. In London this unearned increment is generally admitted to amount to £110,000,-000 in twenty years. It is contended that the persons entitled to this unearned increment are those whose labour and intelligence have created it, and not those who happen to be landowners. The suggestion of the Fabians is, that a municipal death duty of ten per cent be imposed for the purpose of transferring to the people that part of the increased value of land which fairly belongs to them.

2. City guilds : These enjoy an income of £868,-986 a year. They were originally organised to provide for the poor, but now fulfil practically no useful function. It is proposed that they be dissolved, and that the administration of this fund be transferred to the London County Council.

3. Municipalisation of the gas supply : The gas supply of London is in the hands of three companies, of which the largest pays a dividend of twelve per cent. It is proposed that the County Council purchase the works of these three companies at an equitable price, or, in case of refusal of the companies to sell, obtain parliamentary powers to construct a competing system. Manchester, Birmingham, and Bradford are quoted as instances where municipal ownership of gas has resulted in great economy to the taxpayer.

4. Municipalisation of tramways : Tramways in

London are one hundred and twenty-six miles in extent, and in the hands of eleven different companies. They pay a dividend of between seven and ten per cent per annum. The concessions are for a term of twenty-one years, and the city therefore has a right to run the tramways on its own account as fast as the respective concessions expire. The exploitation of tramways by the city has proved successful in Huddersfield; it is therefore demanded that it be tried in London also.

5. London's water supply : London is now provided with water by eight different companies, at a cost of about £700,000 a year. London, however, pays £1,700,000 for the water supply. Nor is the water supplied of good quality, five of the companies deriving it almost entirely from the Thames. It is proposed that the County Council should either purchase these water companies at a fair price, or obtain parliamentary powers to construct a competing supply.

6. London Docks: The London docks have by successive amalgamations fallen into the hands of four companies, which, however, do not succeed in making more than between two and three per cent on their nominal capital. They would probably not make expenses did they not adopt a plan in the employment of labour which, while it saves the companies from bankruptcy, is demoralising and injurious to the interests of the workingman. They only employ a comparatively small staff of regular employees; the bulk of the work is done

by what are termed casuals—that is to say, men who are employed for a day or fraction of a day as the demand for labour requires. This system brings to the docks daily about twenty thousand applicants for work, of which, on an average, seven to eight thousand apply in vain.* The evils of this system are twofold. In the language of Mr. Charles Booth : " The occasional employment of this class of labour by the docks, water-side, and other East-End industries is a gigantic system of outdoor relief. It creates a demoralised and vicious leisure class."† Again, the prevailing notion amongst London workmen is, in their words, that " they can always get a job at the docks." The result of this is, that on the slightest occasion of discontent or temper, or on the slightest temptation to idleness, they abandon regular occupation in order to swell the mob at the dock gates.

For the purpose of putting an end to this demoralising influence, and notwithstanding the fact that as an investment the purchase of the docks would not pay, the Fabian programme asks for the municipalisation of the docks also. The loss, if any, on the docks would be insignificant by the side of the profits that would result from a purchase of other municipal franchises.

7. The markets: Some of the London markets consist of private monopolies operated for the benefit

---

* Mansion House Report, 1886, p. 7.

† Labor in the Life of the People, vol. i, p. 202.

of the owner and not for that of the public. The municipalisation of these markets is demanded.

8. Labour policy: The following demands are made in the interest of labour:

(*a*) A normal eight-hour day for all public employees.

(*b*) Payment of not less than trade-union wages for each occupation.

(*c*) Full liberty of combination.

(*d*) One day's rest in seven, and sufficient holidays.

(*e*) Prohibition of overtime except in unexpected emergencies.

They also demand that the city should employ labour directly, and not work through contractors; or, if in certain cases working through contractors cannot be avoided, that all contracts contain a clause imposing upon the contractor the payment of fair wages.

The above programme is given in its entirety in order to demonstrate that even though some of the demands may be deemed by some excessive, they are on the whole within the range of practical politics; they are not revolutionary, and cannot, even to a conservative eye, seem more unreasonable than any other measure of the Liberal party. It may be objected that a municipal death duty of ten per cent is large, and that full liberty of combination amongst city employees would be dangerous. The recent railroad strikes in Chicago have suggested that steps should be taken to protect the public from the interruption of public service by strikes. It is believed that a system could be devised not unsatisfactory to the workingmen, under which employees in public and quasi-public service should make time contracts which they would not be at liberty to violate, thus giving employers an opportunity of preventing the interruption of service created by sudden refusal on the part of the employees to perform duties on which the public ought to count.* But this very question is one which suggests the importance of socialistic questions being carefully studied by those who are least likely to do so in a hostile spirit. It is not reasonable to suppose that railroad directors can bring to such a question as this the dispassionate study which it deserves; nor is it reasonable to suppose that the workingman will readily adopt the doctrine that the public must be protected from the suddenenss of the interruption upon which the workingman counts in order to secure his terms. The point which must be brought home to the workingman in this connection is that his strikes succeed when they are justified, and when because they are justified, they have the sympathy of the public; that they do not succeed when they are

---

* While these pages are going through the press the State Board of Mediation and Arbitration, in its report upon the trolley strike in Brooklyn, recommends that engagements for a definite period be rendered obligatory on transportation companies, and that resignations or dismissals be not permitted except upon due notice or under extraordinary circumstances.—*See New York Sun, February 8, 1895.*

not justified, and when they do not have the sympathy of the public. In other words, the workman
forms part of a social system which he cannot afford
to mass in opposition to himself. In his own interest, therefore, it is folly so to cripple the public
service as to create indignation in the very quarter
where he needs sympathy. Assuming that the railroad employee is engaged for a term of not less than
six months, and that both he and his employer must
give one another a month's notice before the expiration of the term in case either of them desires to end
the employment, is it not clear that notice given by
five thousand railroad employees that they would
one month ahead cease to work for the railroad, with
a fair and dispassionate statement of the reasons of
such a decision, would command from the public
the support which they need, and be more likely to
bring about a fair adjustment of their demands than
violent interruption of the service, and the scenes of
violence which it is impossible to prevent on such
occasions? It is not contended that railroad employees would readily understand this, but they are
more likely to understand it if some disinterested
person takes the trouble of bringing it home to
them during periods of calm than if it is hurled at
them by indignant employers in the heat of conflict.

It may also be urged by some against the Fabian
programme that ten per cent is too large a death
duty to exact; but the figure has not been set down
as an *ultimatum*, and it is reasonable to suppose

that a fair adjustment of the figure could be arrived at.

In a word, the Fabian programme is comparatively moderate; has certainly nothing in it that is outrageous; nothing in it which does not deserve careful discussion; and it is, perhaps, just because there are features in it which require amendment that it becomes the duty of all those who recognize their responsibility as citizens to understand the problems involved. Such a study would enable the large class of citizens who to-day stand neutral between the employer and the employee to exercise a wholesome influence that would lead to a proper adjustment, and avoid the evils and misery that attend revolt and revolution.

The same thing can be said of the programme of the People's party, to which reference has already been made. This platform demands the following:

1. Free and unlimited coinage of silver and gold at 16 to 1.

2. Increase of circulating medium to not less than fifty dollars *per capita*.

3. Graduated income-tax.

4. "That the money of the country be kept as much as possible in the hands of the people, and the limitation of national revenues to the necessary expenses of the Government."

5. Postal savings banks.

6. Nationalisation of railroads, telegraphs, and telephones.

7. " The land, including all the natural sources
of wealth, is the heritage of the people and should
not be monopolised for speculative purposes, and
alien ownership of land should be prohibited. All
land now held by railroads and other corporations
in excess of their actual needs, and all lands now
owned by aliens, should be reclaimed by the Government and held for actual settlers only."

A discussion of the merits and demerits of this
platform will not be undertaken; but the attention
of all earnest men is directed to the fact that there
is in this programme something that is practicable
and much that is impracticable; that the party
which stands upon this platform is making rapid
progress in the country; that the task of educating
the People's party so as to make it distinguish between those parts of their programme which are
sound from those parts of it which are unsound
cannot be confided to the machines of the Republican and Democratic parties: that the duty of
accomplishing this work must and always will remain in those citizens who appreciate the respon-
sibilities of their franchise; and that while the
necessity of undertaking this work may not seem
considerable to citizens of the Eastern States, they
are of vital importance to those of the West. Nor
can the country at large long remain indifferent to
the issues which vitally concern any important fraction of the people. The passion for cheap money
which prevails in some States is one of the most
amazing political fallacies to which our fellow-citi-

zens are exposed. It is all the more amazing when
we find it entertained by the very men who would
suffer most from the folly of adopting it, for while
the dollar would cheapen, wages would remain the
same. It is the men who understand what money is
who would be the first to modify their business arrangements accordingly. The large monopolists and
bankers would take care to lose least, and possibly
in some cases profit by the change; whereas, those
whose ignorance of the subject is evidenced by the
very fact that they demand a depreciated coinage
that would impoverish them, are the very ones who
would be the last to know how to accommodate
themselves to it. The most elementary explanation
that money represents purchasing power, and that
its value to an individual depends upon its purchasing power and not upon the Government stamp
which is put upon it, ought to suffice to puncture
the folly of this demand. But if this explanation
is offered by one who is politically opposed to the
members of the People's party, his arguments would
be believed to be founded upon interest, and would
never penetrate the prejudices in favour of cheap
money, or reach that part of the brain which is
capable of coming to an intelligent conclusion.
The question of education will be more fully considered in the following chapter. Meanwhile we
are confronted with the fact that the working people of this land are gradually acquiring political
convictions which contain much that is true and
much that is not true. Every one of those millions

has as much to say at the polls as the most skilful political economist in the country. He does not read from books of political economy; he reads the newspapers. He does not read the newspapers that are politically opposed to him; he reads the newspapers which mirror and exaggerate his own opinions. He wields a power which, when he learns how to exercise it, is great enough to wreck the entire social fabric, and put civilisation back where it was when the sands of the Sahara were allowed to bury the monuments of Egypt. On every man who has a head to understand these questions, and who has a heart to wish them solved for the benefit of his country and to the diminution of the misery of his fellow-creatures, lies the responsibility of taking the steps necessary to see that the great working force of the nation is directed to its advancement and not to its destruction.

The question of socialism cannot be left without treating that aspect of it which brings it into contrast with what is called individualism. It is perfectly consistent with the whole of Herbert Spencer's philosophy that he should be an individualist—that is to say, that he should believe that the present condition of competition is the best possible, and that through individual instinct and the struggle for existence it involves, is there likely to be the greatest chance of improvement for man. Mr. Spencer believes that our present conditions are the inevitable result of the implacable application of cause and effect working through millions of years. He has also satisfied himself that the same principles of evolution that, working in the past, have brought man to where he is to-day, will, working in the future, bring him to an era of universal peace and unselfishness. The principle of determinism, which makes a man the mere puppet of the greater inclination, is a part of the theory that he has been and always will be the product of evolution, over which he has practically no control. So satisfied is Mr. Spencer with these conditions that he is averse to any human interference in the matter. With extraordinary skill and sagacity he has picked out the numerous occasions when legislative interference has produced effects diametrically the reverse of those which it was intended to produce, and has argued from these disappointments against legislative interference in all matters save those referring to protection from violence to life and property. Individualism demands the minimum of state interference ; socialism demands the maximum of state interference. In this respect, therefore, they stand diametrically opposed ; and it becomes necessary, when discussing the subject of socialism, to come to some conclusion regarding them.

In an admirable essay on this subject Mr. D. G. Ritchie, quoting Sir J. Fitzjames Stephen,* propounds three questions as applicable to all legislation:

---

* Liberty, Equality, Fraternity, 1854, 5th edition.

" 1. Is the object aimed at good? that is to say, does it tend to advance the well-being of the community?

" 2. Will the proposed means attain it?

" 3. Will they attain it at too great an expense, or not? that is to say, can the end be obtained without doing more harm than is compensated by the benefit of its attainment?"

By applying these questions to state regulation of opinion, education, agriculture, and industry, he demonstrates very clearly that the question of state interference cannot be decided upon general philosophic grounds, but must be determined in very case upon the merits of the case itself. He points out that as regards the state regulation of opinion, whereas it is undoubtedly improper for the state to attempt to deal with religious opinions where those religious opinions are not such as to jeopardise the prosperity of the country, the state has an undoubted right to regulate the conduct of the people in so far as it is determined by religious opinions that are dangerous to the community. He points out that there are certain people who sincerely believe vaccination to be a poison and a calamity, and who regard compulsory vaccination as persecution :

" Now the difference between such cases and religious persecution is this: There are available statistics about the relation between vaccination and immunity from smallpox, and, if necessary, better statistics can be procured; but theological experts can produce no similarly trustworthy statis-

tics—statistics of a kind that should satisfy a
parliamentary commission—about the relation between orthodoxy (of any given species) and immunity from damnation. Therefore the state does
well if it acts on the wise principle laid down—but,
unfortunately, not always followed by Tiberius:—
' Deorum injuriæ dis curæ'—Wrongs against God
are God's affairs. Or let both state and society listen
to Gamaliel : ' Refrain from these men, and let
them alone : for if this counsel or this work be of
men, it will be overthrown ; but if it is of God, ye
will not be able to overthrow them ; lest haply ye be
found even to be fighting against God." Or let them
listen to a greater than Gamaliel, who said, " Forbid
him not, though he followeth not with us."

It cannot therefore be laid down that there is
any hard-and-fast rule as to whether the state should
interfere with opinion or not. Whether it is wise
and proper to do so must always remain a question
of great difficulty, and can be answered only by the
peculiar conditions which each case presents.

Another illustration of this subject is furnished
by the action of the French Republic in expelling
Jesuits. This undoubtedly was an act which might
be properly characterised as religious persecution,
and yet it is probable that the republic would not
have survived if it had failed to adopt this course.
The Jesuits were daily engaged in inculcating into
the youth of France a spirit of religious hostility to
republican forms of government, and cultivating in
them loyalty to those monarchical institutions from

the destruction of which the Roman Church has
itself so profoundly suffered. Although at a time
when the republic was struggling for its very life
against monarchical reaction it may be thought
proper for it to have adopted a course which undoubtedly trespassed severely upon principles of
individual liberty precious to every republican heart,
it was one upon which republicans themselves were
at the time divided. Undoubtedly in America those
who thought at all about the subject were disposed
to censure the French Government for the course it
then pursued; and yet many who have followed the
events of French politics closely during the last
twenty years are satisfied that a failure on the part
of the French Republic to protect itself by such a
measure would probably have ended before this in
the restoration of some reactionary form of government, and in the indefinite postponement of the enjoyment of that very personal liberty which these
measures seemed so ruthlessly to attack.

In the same connection Professor Huxley asks
whether the English Government was wrong in suppressing Thuggee in India,* and adopts the dictum
of Locke, that " the end of government is the good of
mankind "; from which it follows as the night the
day that wherever the state can wisely legislate so
as to increase the good or diminish the evil in the
world such legislation cannot be other than a blessing. In this conclusion Professor Huxley remains

* Methods and Results; Administrative Nihilism, p. 279.

consistent with his theory before explained, that man is engaged in a struggle with Nature and is not doomed to compliance with it.

The foregoing considerations suffice to indicate generally the character of the problem presented by socialism, the necessity of handling it, and the mistake that underlies the theory of individualism, which would fain waive it to one side as unworthy of any consideration whatever.

If the reader will imagine himself for one moment the autocrat of the United States, he will not hesitate to recognise the imperative duty that would be incumbent upon him to study and come to a definite conclusion upon labour questions which touch so nearly the lives of a large majority of his subjects. His throne, his life itself, would depend upon the wisdom of its solution. Now the task which he would undertake in order to save his throne and person, popular government imposes upon every voter in order to save his political freedom and keep whole the civilisation in which he lives. There is to-day among the well-to-do a growing concern in the municipal problem ; but the problem of socialism is still left unconsidered, partly because it is not seen to concern them, and partly because it is believed to have been disposed of by the sweeping generalisations of individualism and *laissez-faire*.

As a matter of fact, socialism presents two very different aspects from different points of view : one is theoretical, the other practical. Theoretically

socialism represents the war between the collectivist
and the individualist; practically it presents a
series of demands for state interference. As regards
its theoretical side, it is not because socialism indulges
in hopes of a millennium that it is necessarily foolish
or extreme. The heaven of Christianity is not less
unattainable than the ultimate hopes of the socialist;
and yet Christianity serves its purpose in the world.
To a practical student the problem presented by socialism is one of state interference. Now it has
been shown that the advisableness of state interference is a question which can only be decided for
every issue that invokes it; that the state interference demanded by socialists is not revolutionary;
that it is, perhaps, to some extent immediately practicable. Surely, if this be so it deserves to be
considered by us without prejudice or passion, if we
would save the state from the explosiveness of popular excitement too long pent up.

Once the people get to believe that their wrongs
spring from evils that can be cured by the state, and
once they begin to organise with a view to political
action, we can no longer oppose to them the opinions
of the *doctrinaire*. This conviction of the people
is a fact with which we have to deal; and the way to
deal with it is not to smile at it with derision, but to
study it with conscience and care, yielding all we
wisely can, and, by conceding to just demands,
strengthen ourselves to meet those demands that are
foolish or unjust.

Now this task is one of education.
15

CHAPTER XII.

THE PROBLEM OF EDUCATION.

No one can travel throughout the West without being profoundly impressed by the fact that in every village, though its stores, hotels, national banks, and town hall itself, are relegated to structures of wood, there is one conspicuous building of substantial brick, and this building is the schoolhouse. There is no doubt but that the country we live in is, relatively to its space and population, as well provided with schools for primary education as any country in the world. Every city has, of course, its local problem of education to solve. One is vexed by the religious question; another is hampered by insufficient appropriations; a third, by appointment made for political service instead of educational qualifications; a fourth, by a system of administration that is needlessly complicated. New York would not live up to its primacy in misgovernment if it lacked any one of these four. But into the abuses and evils that arise from these sources it is not proposed to enter: for this work is not so much engaged in the study of political abuses themselves as in the relation of these abuses to the citizen; in the source and reason of them; and particularly in the rôle that religious effort can play in diminishing them. The defects in the municipal administration of our charities have been studied in some detail because it is in our charities that religious men are particularly interested, because private charity can never do more than merely supplement state charity, and in state charity, therefore, must always remain the lion's share of the work; and, lastly, because the deficiencies in the working of this department in New York illustrate the impossibility of securing good administration of a good law so long as the administration is confided to a corrupt political machine. The examination of the other departments of municipal government would only reveal still more startling abuses, all tending towards the same conclusion. It would be waste of time for the purposes of this work to enumerate them.

But there is a wider view of the question of education which demands the serious consideration of every earnest citizen. No one will dispute the contention that a knowledge of reading, writing, and arithmetic, such as is given in primary schools, is not sufficient to equip a man for the solution of the political and economical problems which on every election day he is called upon to solve; and yet we have to confront the undoubted fact that the large majority of our citizens are expected to solve these problems without any more equipment than this, and are armed with a vote which puts every one of

them on every election day on a par with the most
distinguished authority on political economy in the
country. The fact is, that the primary education,
which is all that the majority of our fellow-citizens
enjoy, does no more than fit them for reading the
newspapers; and that the great educator in the
country is not the primary school, is not the board
of education, is not the Church—it is the press.
Indeed, one may go further, and say that the press is
the great instrument of education not only for our
uneducated but for our educated classes; for it is
from the newspaper alone that the busy man derives
his knowledge of the events of the day, and it is
practically impossible for him to get information
from any other source. It therefore becomes of extraordinary importance to consider carefully just
what is the education which our fellow-citizens are
receiving therefrom.

It is the fashion to abuse the newspapers. One
of them, which is the recognised organ in New York
of Tammany Hall, is described as making vice attractive; another, which ranks amongst the first for
holding up a high standard in politics, is described
as making virtue repulsive; so that whether the
tendency of a newspaper is to degrade or to improve
the community, both come in for universal censure.
As a matter of fact, the press of New York, with the
single exception already referred to, has for years
been unanimously hostile to Tammany Hall. Col-
ums have been devoted every day to the revelation
of abuses in Tammany Hall and to appeals to the

citizens for united action against it.   If the citizens
of the city of New York were as active in their opposition to Tammany Hall as its newspapers, Tammany Hall would have long since been wiped out of
existence.   The same thing is true in other cities.
It is undoubtedly true in Chicago, where the public
spirit of the newspapers seems to far exceed that of
the voting population.   Fairness obliges us to admit
that the press of this country, taken as a whole, is
financially uncorrupted and incorruptible.   So far,
then, it would seem as though the press could be
relied upon to hold up a high standard of political
virtue to the citizen.   Unfortunately, however, there
are elements which enter into the publication of
newspapers which disqualify them as educators, and
make them all the more dangerous as such because,
as a matter of fact, most of them are generally believed to be, and probably are, unpurchasable in the
commonly accepted use of the word.   These two
elements are competition and partisanship.

Let us consider, first, the effect of competition on
the educational qualifications of the press.   Newspapers are not run for educational purposes; they
are run for commercial purposes; they are money-
making enterprises, in no way differing in this respect from a bank or an insurance or other trading
company.   There are, of course, exceptional editors
who take a sufficient personal pride in their papers
to prefer morality to commercial returns.   It is
doubtless some such sentiment as this that maintains the high standard of the press in England.   It

is probably also this that tends to keep the standard
high in America; but, unfortunately, the majority of
editors are driven by the struggle for life to sacrifice
everything to the commercial feature; and the
presence in the community of a single paper successfully run on these lines is sufficient to render the
task of holding up a high standard in the press
difficult, if not impossible. Margaret Fuller has
said that "while one man remains base no man can
be altogether great." This is particularly true in
journalism. So long as an editor has to meet expenses he has to meet the methods employed by the
most successful of his competitors. If the most
successful of his competitors keeps the standard low,
the latter has an easier task in breaking down the
standard than the former in elevating it, for there
are more readers in a city who love scandal—especially when the scandal is illustrated—than there
are men who want trustworthy information on
questions involving political economy and the general good. The editor, therefore, who succeeds in
capturing the approval of the mass and securing a
large circulation controls the largest amount of
advertisements and the highest prices therefor;
for the advertiser seeks to reach the largest public, and therefore advertises most advantageously
in the papers having the largest circulation. In
this way the successful editor cuts into the business
of his rivals in their two most vulnerable points:
he cuts into their sales by withdrawing from
them their readers, and he cuts into the proceeds

from advertisements by the reputation of a large circulation.

The methods of the successful American editor of to-day consist chiefly in furnishing the public with perpetual subjects of excitement; and, unfortunately, the public seems more interested in a divorce in high life than in the effect of legislation upon our finances. The result is, that more and more attention is given to scandal, and less and less to those matters which it is most important that the citizen should learn. This perpetual feast of scandal reacts upon the public, which becomes more and more exacting of this sort of pabulum. The ordinary events of the day do not furnish sufficient interest for the satisfaction of the ever-increasing demand of the public. Scandals have therefore to be created, and newspapers now devote themselves to the preparation of "stories" which are of a character to interest and excite the public mind. Now, of the stories so prepared and written up, some of them occasionally strike an abuse of great interest to the public, and in so far as they do, the public is interested in being fully informed regarding the same; but if one newspaper has started an investigation into a particular abuse, no other newspaper will give the matter any attention. All the other newspapers wage against it a war of silence. The evil consequence of this system is obvious. A man would have to read all the newspapers in a city in order to be sure that he was being informed of all the events which are of interest to him therein. Quite recently one of the prominent papers in the city of New York started an investigation into one of our large public institutions. The investigation turned out to be of the greatest interest; it unearthed abuses of the most serious character; yet such was the silence of the other papers on the subject that none but the readers of the paper which started the investigation were ever informed regarding it except in the most cursory and insufficient manner. On the other hand, if a newspaper starts a cry against any of our institutions which turns out not to be justified, it considers its reputation at stake in the matter and endeavours to make good its charges. If it has a large enough circulation it secures investigation by legislative committees, and has been known to obtain a report in its favour in spite of the fact that the original charges were quite unfounded. This is being demonstrated now regarding one of the most meritorious institutions in all the United States of America, and perhaps of its kind in the world. There is a maxim among newspaper men that no newspaper can ever afford to admit that it has been in the wrong. As to the morality of this maxim little need be said; as to its application there cannot possibly be any doubt; and some excuse must be made for editors, in view of the fact that many of them are engaged in a veritable struggle for existence. Now, if a manufacturer were asked to admit that his wares were inferior to those of a competitor, it is not likely that he would be induced to do so. This is what an editor is called upon to do when he

is asked to correct a mistake, and that mistake has
been pointed out by one of his "esteemed contemporaries."

The fact is that newspapers are not run for the
purpose of education; they are run for the purpose
of profit; and although an editor may be willing to
adopt an unpopular course when it is a mere question of lessening rather than increasing profits, he
cannot be expected to adopt a course that will not
only destroy profits altogether but incur loss. A
newspaper therefore cannot adopt a truly independent policy unless it enjoys a degree of financial
prosperity which is extremely rare, and, under existing conditions, can hardly be obtained except by
methods totally inconsistent with a high standard.

It is not competition only, however, which has
disqualified the press for the task of education which
it has unconsciously assumed. In one sense of the
word competition tends to keep newspapers up to
the mark in the furnishing of accurate news. Partisanship, on the other hand, is habitually engaged in
furnishing the public with inaccurate news, or with
news so garbled in passing through the spectacles
of partisanship that by the time an editor turns it
over to the public it no longer presents the facts
as they are. It would be impossible to take up any
collection of morning papers published in one city
without finding illustrations of this. Thus, on the
day on which these lines are written,* one promi-

* November 16, 1894.

nent New York paper publishes the following head-
lines:

"The World was right: Democrats may dispute
the validity of all laws passed next winter."

And another, on the same day, publishes with
reference to the same incident the following:

"Constitutionality of the Legislature after January 1st. Lawyers of both parties agree with substantial unanimity that the validity of its acts cannot
successfully be attacked."

The inconsistency between these two statements
can hardly be greater. When account is taken of
the fact that most men have only time to read one
paper in the day, and that men generally read the
paper which represents the political party to which
they belong, the extent of the evil attending a partisan press can be appreciated. One who reads a
Republican newspaper never knows the arguments
that can be made in favour of free trade; and one
who reads a Democratic paper never knows the
arguments that can be made in favour of protection. The members of each party are therefore more
and more confirmed in their views, and more and
more separated from one another. To those who are
thoroughly grounded in political economy this evil
is somewhat attenuated, provided the education has
been sufficiently thorough to resist the daily dose
of theoretical doctrine, and the man himself is sufficiently strong to distinguish between what is sound
and what is unsound in the partisan arguments presented. But to a man who has had no education in

political economy, and who derives his principles as
well as his facts from the same prejudiced source,
there is practically no opportunity for a change or
modification of opinion.

This is the explanation of the amazing success
of some economic fallacies in the country—as, for
example, the demand for cheap money which expressed itself some years ago as the greenback fal-
lacy, and which is expressed now in the demand for
an unlimited issue of depreciated coin. Again, the
Democratic press is engaged in endeavouring to persuade the people that all commercial and industrial
depression comes from the mistakes of the Republicans ; and the Republicans are engaged in endeavouring to persuade the people that all commercial
and industrial depression comes through the mistakes
of the Democrats. The principal issue between these
two parties is that of the tariff, and thus the mind
of the people is directed away from financial legislation, which is perhaps the chief culprit. If to-mor-
row the Populists were to have their way, and were
to obtain legislation of a character to give them the
cheap money they ask for, when they began to suffer from the consequence of this legislation, the aim
of one party would be to attribute the trouble to
protection, the aim of the other party would be to
attribute the trouble to free trade, and the real
cause of the trouble would stand a good chance of
escaping detection altogether.

But this is by no means the worst side of the
subject. Under every representative form of gov-

ernment the vote is cast rather for men than for measures. The mass, under existing conditions of education, does not feel itself competent to vote on complicated questions of finance and economics, but it does understand, or thinks it understands, the merits of individual candidates. On this subject, however, as well as upon questions of political and economic principles, it is the political duty of the partisan press to persistently mislead its readers. The basest motives are regularly ascribed to every public man for every important vote he casts, so that it is impossible for any one in public life to command the respect of more than those of the party to which he belongs, with the exception, of course, of the comparatively few who have the leisure to read the organs of more than one political party. Calumny has become so general that the public can no longer distinguish between that which is founded and that which is unfounded; and so, while every public man is rendered contemptible by the press, the evil done by those who deserve censure is over-looked because the charge of having done evil is generally believed to be prompted by the animosity of partisanship. The result of this is that the public do not know what to believe, and end by be-lieving nothing; so that when a man wants to con-vey the fact that a rumour is false, he says that he read it in some newspaper.

And yet nothing can be more unfair to news-papers than this, for, with the exception of such matter as comes within the range of partisan politics and the errors that come from unskilful reporting upon events of secondary importance, nothing can exceed the enterprise and general accuracy with which American newspapers collect and publish news. The public, however, is characteristically unfair, and, by an unintelligent application of the principle, *falsus in uno falsus in omnibus*, it readily looks with suspicion on all it reads; whereas with an unconscious discrimination it knows very well how to separate that matter which can be believed from that which must be taken *cum grano salis*. The point, however, which must be kept carefully in mind is, that the very matters concerning which it is most important that the public should be well informed are those regarding which the newspapers are least to be trusted.

The exact hour of the Czar's death, the squabbles of the doctors about his bedside, the arrangements of his funeral, are all reported with astonishing detail and accuracy, although they are matters of no importance to the American citizen in respect to his political duties; whereas an event as important as the great strike in Chicago is described with such partiality towards the strikers in one set of newspapers, and such partiality towards the companies in another set, that one class in the community believes each, and the other believes neither—ignorance, prejudice, or confusion being the net result for all.

And if this be the case as regards a subject which involves no party question, how much more is it the case when such questions are involved. Shortly after the McKinley tariff was enacted a war arose amongst the papers as regards the question whether there had arisen in the country since the enactment any factories of tin plate. One New York paper asserted positively that there had, gave the names of the owners, the names of the places, and the amount of the output. Another New York paper, on the other hand, stated with vehemence that there were no such factories, and that the output was a pure fiction of the brain. As regards this question the public is still uninformed. This is, of course, only offered as an example. Such examples could be multiplied *ad nauseam.*

Now it is submitted that the merits of such an event as the Chicago strike are of capital importance to a true understanding of the labour question; and yet to-day the public is so divided on the subject that one half of the community regards its leader, Debs, as a prophet and martyr, whereas the other half regard him as a wicked dipsomaniac. Nor could there be a more necessary factor in the practical decision of the merits of protection and free trade respectively than a true answer to the question, Does protection protect?—and yet the readers of one paper are persuaded that in the case of the tin-plate industry a high tariff did create an otherwise impossible industry, whereas the readers of the opposition sheet are taught that no industry can be created even by a prohibitively protective tariff under any circumstances whatever.

That the press should argue from facts to conclusions is altogether right and proper; but that it should garble facts to bolster theories is—so long as the press is our principal educator — nothing less than a national calamity; for such a course not only deprives the public of the facts which are indispensable to the framing of a conclusion, but actually drives it to an erroneous conclusion by what is nothing short of a betrayal of confidence.

And here we touch the ethical question involved in this question of education. The work of the journalist is not a purely money-making business; it includes a great trust, and one which citizens can no longer afford to leave to the accidents of competition and partisanship. We do not leave the education of our children to unchecked private enterprise. We have recognised the importance to the State of having our children all know how to read and write, and we have therefore adopted the socialist plan of providing State education for them. Nor is higher education left to the accidents of private competition; citizens have been found generous enough to found universities and scholarships, so that an intelligent youth can to-day in America secure an education of the highest order at a practically nominal figure compared with what it really costs, and some few can obtain it free of all charge whatever. The principle that education must be endowed is conceded both as regards primary and higher education : that it should be endowed as re-

gards the daily education of our sovereign citizens
is only a further step in the same direction.

It is a hopeful sign of the advance of moral
ideas which Mr. Kidd has lately so well described,
that what was of old regarded as private property
is more and more getting to be regarded as a public
trust. Before 1789 office was regarded in France as
the appanage of the king and nobles; certain families owned certain offices, with a tenure as recognised as that of their castles and their coats of
arms. The idea that the people had any interest in
the wise, economical, and public-spirited administration of public office would at that time have
seemed far more grotesque and impractical than to-
day that the public had any interest in the wise and
public-spirited administration by a Vanderbilt or
Astor of the wealth which the accumulation of
several generations has handed down to him. It
has taken several revolutions to break down in
France this aristocratic notion of property in public
office, and from these revolutions the whole world
has profited. Public office a public trust, has become in America a maxim, the truth of which no
man would dare publicly to deny, however contemptuously it may be privately derided by the practical
politician. Nor is the idea that private wealth can
in any sense constitute a public trust more foreign
to the present generation than was the trust theory
of public office to that which preceded the French
Revolution. The theory has been openly advocated,
not only by socialists and positivists but by a literary

millionaire himself. The recognition that journalism also constitutes a public trust is along the same line of moral advancement.

The great difficulty in the way of applying this principle to the journalism of to-day consists in the two obstacles to faithful journalism which have been already pointed out—namely, partisanship and commercial competition. Of the former, more will be said in the next chapter; of the latter, little more need be added than that it can only be met in one way—endowment.

If a great newspaper were started in any of the large cities in this country under the same conditions as its principal universities, there is some chance that the public would be provided with information regarding the subjects of the day, upon the accuracy of which they could depend. This suggestion must not be understood as a contention that endowment would solve all the problems presented by the existing defects in our press. An endowed press would be as likely to fall into evil hands as an endowed religion, and far more likely to fall into evil hands than an endowed university. A weapon against evil such as an endowed press would be, as long as it remained in the hands of those whose public spirit had endowed it, cannot be disparaged by the argument that this weapon might fall into the hands of the enemy. Such an argument applied to national defences would prevent us from ever building a fort or a man-of-war. As long as evil exists it will have to be fought, and it

16

will have to be fought with weapons that are commensurate with it. If our hands are too weak to hold the weapons we forge in order to defeat it, we must trust that in a new generation stronger hands will be found to wield still more perfect weapons. It is the history of almost every organization constituted for the purpose of warring against evil that it tends ultimately to take the side of evil against those who constituted it. It would therefore be a mistake to imagine that because an endowed press might ultimately join the ranks of the enemy we must not endow a press at all. We find ourselves to-day confronted with an evil which is open, flagrant, and unchecked. It is difficult to conceive how, so long as commercial competition determines the character of our press, it can rise much above the level which it now occupies. The only remedy, therefore, seems to be to lift it out of the necessities of competition by endowment.

One of the dangers to which an endowed press would be most exposed is that of becoming *doctrinaire*. This danger can be avoided by adopting the plan of publishing articles on both sides of every important subject. It should not be forgotten that the great function of such a press ought to be to furnish facts; these facts should be furnished uncolored by bias, whether religious or partisan; from. these facts the exponents of the different factions or parties ought to be allowed freely to argue in a column of the paper devoted to that purpose. Such a paper would be divided into two strongly differentiated parts : one part would be devoted to the collection of news, and the facts given therein would be collected with the care and dispassionateness that mark the lecture hall of a university ; the other part would consist of signed articles by recognised authorities and representatives of existing parties, each drawing his conclusion from the facts, and, if necessary, challenging the facts themselves.

The editorial column would be sparingly used, and devoted mainly to the task of summing up.

It might not be necessary or prudent to publish such a newspaper daily ; it would probably better serve the purpose for which it was published if it only appeared once a week, and in such a shape that it could be bound, so as to serve as a continuous record of current events. Such a publication need not be extremely costly. The collection of foreign news, which constitutes a large part of the expense of daily papers, could with safety be left to the existing members of the press, the principal object of endowment being to educate the citizen regarding those matters which concern him at home.

The existence of so admirable a weekly as The Nation is not an argument against the publication of such a paper as the one proposed ; for the proposed weekly would make a point of containing the local information which is conspicuously absent from the columns of The Nation. It is doubtful whether The Nation, the circulation of which is derived from the whole country, could be made to pay were a large part of its space devoted to local information regarding the operations of city departments. And yet this is the information which it is the duty of every New York citizen to procure, and which to-day he is without the means of procuring save at the cost of more time than he can afford to spare from his business occupations.

The university of every large city could undoubtedly be enlisted in support of such endowment, and the public be thereby kept informed regarding every important item of interest, whether in science, in sociology, in political economy, in medicine, or in law. Were it known that such information emanated from the pen of a university professor and was published under the responsibility of the university to which he belonged, value would be attached to it which cannot be allowed to matter of the same kind now published in Sunday editions. It must not be supposed that it is advised to confide the editing of such a paper to a university or to the faculty of a university. Its editors must be men as thoroughly equipped for journalism as those who now edit the great papers of the country; but as regards those subjects which can best be dealt with by men whose special duty it is to keep informed regarding them through the business of lecturing upon them to which they devote their lives, it is submitted that the university faculty could render signal service. Nor must the above suggestion be supposed to imply that an endowed paper would immediately secure the confidence of the community; it would have to win its way just

as any other paper, though it would have in its
favour the fact of financial independence and the
co-operation of a staff such as no other newspaper
in the country could command.   Such a paper
would not in any sensible degree affect the circulation of existing papers, for it would furnish its information only once a week, and it would seek to be
free from that partisanship which makes the sale of
most of those now on the market.   Moreover, it
would undertake to publish matter that would not
commercially pay, and abstain from publishing matter which is cheap and popular.   At any rate, were
such a paper in existence it ought to be possible for
a citizen to know the facts upon which he is called
upon to express his opinion ; it ought to be possible for him to understand the working of the city
departments without having to sift this information out of the unintelligible columns of the city
records ; and he ought at any rate to be left without excuse if he failed to know the issues upon
which he is required to vote.   By such an endowment, education would not stop short at a moment
when for the purposes of good citizenship it is most
needed, but would extend through adolescence to
every day of a busy man's life.   That it would
serve to greatly facilitate and shorten the labour of
getting information of current events, will be admitted by those who now laboriously sift it out of
the columns of many newspapers ; and all whose
occupations make it impossible for them to read
more than one paper a day cannot but recognise

that it would serve as an admirable antidote to the
dose of prejudice which they now daily consume.
Nor can it be believed that it would fail to have
a beneficent influence upon its contemporaries.
While commercial competition is acting to drag
down the general standard, such a paper could not
but do something to hold that standard up; it
would, at all events, serve to inculcate the great
moral lesson that journalism, like public office and
inherited wealth, cannot any longer be regarded as
private property, but must be recognised to involve
a solemn trust.

CHAPTER XIII.

PARTY GOVERNMENT.

PARTISANSHIP is at once the mainspring of popular government and its bane. No great issue has ever been pushed to a conclusion until it has either created a party or been adopted by one already in existence; but just in the same way as the human institution to which religion gives rise and through which it operates, by falling into the hands of designing men, tends to defeat the very object for which it was organised, so the machinery necessary to the propagation of a political idea, however sound, tends to outlive the issue for which it was constructed, in order to serve private ends at the expense of the common weal. It has been already pointed out that the Republican party, organised for the purpose of suppressing slavery and resisting the exorbitant demands of the subsequently seceding States, perpetuated itself in power by keeping alive sectional animosity; and after it was defeated upon this issue, restored itself to power by promising the labourer high wages under a protective tariff, thereby substituting an entirely new issue for the original one which brought it into existence.

237

Whether or not the Republican party was justified in continuing to appeal to Northern sentiment against the South long after the South had, to all appearances, laid down its arms, it is clear that the temptation to do so would be irresistible if unscrupulous party managers thought that they could thereby maintain themselves in power; and although there undoubtedly is a remote connection between protective tariff and strong central government, it is difficult to believe that the party created for pushing the issue concluded by the war was in any sense obliged by its convictions to take up the cause of protection. It is much easier to believe that the cause of protection was taken up by those in control of the Republican machine because it was an issue likely to furnish them with the funds and popularity indispensable to their maintenance in power. And so the machinery of party organisation constructed for the purpose of advocating the cause of liberty and patriotism was made to serve the private purposes of a few political leaders. This estimate of the course pursued by the Republican party may seem unfair to those who believe as sincerely in protection as they did before in the abolition of slavery and the maintenance of the Union; to these, however, it is respectfully submitted that it is quite possible for others of their fellow-citizens to have been as earnest as themselves in their desire for the abolition of slavery and for the maintenance of the Union, and yet to be equally sincere in their belief in free trade. These have a right to protest against the glorious successes of the Republican party upon the field of battle, upon the field of politics, and upon the field of finance being now converted to the use of those who desire to advocate a theory that has no necessary connection with the real issues of the war.

But whatever may be the evils attending partisanship, the idea of abolishing it must be definitely abandoned. Man is born with an instinct of partisanship which he has acquired from gregarious ancestors; it is a part of the herding faculty, and consists of two very opposite dispositions: one, the disposition to obey a recognised leader, and the other, a willingness to sacrifice one's own opinions for the common good. Both are called into play in every political emergency, and both appeal to the most servile as well as the most independent of our fellow-citizens.

There is, however, a very marked difference between party government as it is understood in Europe and party government as it is understood in America. In the former, partisanship is determined by a temperamental difference which finds its roots deep down in the character of man; whereas, in America, party lines have arisen irrespective of temperament, and for the purpose of meeting a particular emergency. Thus an Englishman or a Frenchman is born a Conservative or he is born a Liberal; or, if he is not born with partisan convictions, he acquires them under conditions which make them colour his view of all political questions.

It is impossible to conceive of a Conservative taking
anything but a conservative view of the subject of
the abolition of the House of Lords; it is impossible to conceive of a Liberal taking anything but a
liberal view on the subject of the education of the
working classes; and conversion from the ranks of
one party to those of the other only takes place
when the parties respectively force views on their
partisans more extreme than the whole body is willing to accept. Conservatism and liberalism are
rendered possible in Europe because Europe has a
history, and because it has institutions which have
grown slowly up under the sanction of that history.
The desire to cling to existing institutions and the
existing order of things is the characteristic of the
Conservative; the desire to innovate and reform is
the characteristic of the Liberal. This profound
difference of temperament will prompt an opposite
view of almost every political question that can be
imagined; for every issue suggests a change, and
those who are temperamentally disposed to innovate tend to favour the change, while those who are
temperamentally disposed to maintain the *status
quo* will oppose the change. Here, therefore, the
line is drawn deep down in human character: the
distinction between the two parties is one that exists
whether there be party government or not, and one
which will determine the existence of parties in
Europe whatever be the form of government.

The comparative youth of the United States of
America takes away the very foundation upon which

the distinction between conservatism and liberalism rests. The only thing which we have to preserve is our Constitution, and this no one to speak of desires to attack.

Attempt has been made to maintain that all opposing parties in the United States have divided along the same line, those on one side of the line favouring a strict construction of the Constitution, and those on the other side of the line favouring a liberal construction of the Constitution. If such a contention could be justified it would support the theory that in America, as well as in England, party lines are drawn along lines of temperament; the strict constructionist would be the Tory, the liberal constructionist would be the Radical; but the contention cannot be maintained. Whenever the strict constructionists have got into power and have found it necessary to justify their use of power by a liberal construction of the Constitution, they have become liberal constructionists; whenever, on the other hand, the liberal constructionists have been thrown out of power they have, in their desire to condemn the administration, become strict constructionists. Examples of this are familiar to every student of American history. Jefferson, who was the leader of the strict constructionists before he was elected to the presidency, strained the Constitution more than any other President that had preceded or has followed him, in order to justify the purchase of Louisiana; and those who had preceded him in power, and whose liberal construction he had himself re-

hemently attacked, became the strictest of constructionists when opposition forced them into an attitude of criticism. The fact is that the party in
power is always the liberal constructionist, and the
party in opposition always the strict constructionist.

There is another fundamental difference between
party government on different sides of the Atlantic.
In England and France party government is recognised by the Constitution ; the permanent Executive is a nominal office ; the real Executive is in the
ministry and shifts with the majority in the Legislature. In England, the Queen does little more than
register the decisions of her parliament ; in France,
the Executive is never at liberty to sign an executive
document without the countersignature of a minister responsible to the Chamber ; * in both cases the
real Executive is the ministry; in both cases the real
Executive depends for its existence upon the party
which is supported by a majority in the Lower
House.

In the United States a totally different principle prevails. Instead of allowing the Executive to
shift with every vote in Congress, we have adopted
the plan of electing our Executive for a definite
term of four years; and this permanent Executive
exercises an influence upon legislation such as is
unknown in England and in France. In France,
the Executive has practically no veto ; he can do no

---

* Loi Constitutionnelle du 25 Fev., 1875, art. 4.

more than ask the Legislature to reconsider its decision ; * in England, though the Queen has in theory a right of veto she has for many years refrained from exercising it. The veto power which the Executive exercises in the United States converts it into a third chamber, and the effect of electing a President with this power for four years is practically to determine the policy of the country during those four years, by subjecting that policy to the veto of the President elected. Under this system there is no change of government every time the majority shifts in the Legislature. The existence of a party and party leader necessitated by the English and French plan does not exist, and therefore the existence of parties is not recognised in the Constitution.

Under these conditions the question may well be asked, What necessity is there for the existence of parties in the United States at all? And this question is one which deserves the attention of all those interested in the survival of popular government.

A brief reference to party history in the beginning of the century will serve to answer it. At the risk of wearying those who are already familiar with this subject, it may be well to recapitulate the history of the rise and fall of the Federal, Whig, and Republican parties, if only to call attention to the practical possibility of governing the country

---

* Loi Constitutionnelle du 25 Fev., 1872, art. 7.

without any party, in the absence of an issue important enough to render a party necessary.

Everybody is familiar with the two elements of opinion which existed at the time the Constitution was adopted, and which found their advocates respectively in Hamilton on the one side and Jefferson on the other. The one favoured strong central Government, the other favoured State rights; the one derived his political convictions from England, then under the rule of a strong permanent Executive, and the other from France, then engaged in a deadly battle with the throne. Jefferson's party were called Republicans, Hamilton's were called Federalists. Washington, desiring to ignore the existence of these two hostile factions, constructed his Cabinet equally of both, and hoped in that way to prevent the predominance of either. In this last he was mistaken: the Federalists kept the upper hand until the election of Jefferson, during whose administration the original issues were practically forgotten in the more burning immediate question whether the country should side with France or England in the war then raging between them. As has been already said, Jefferson, in his desire to maintain strong local government against strong central government, had inveighed bitterly against every attempt of the Federalists to extend their power, but as soon as he was elected to the presidential chair he interpreted his own powers far more largely than ever had Washington, Madison, or Adams; it cannot therefore be conscientiously said that the question either of a strong central government or a strict protective tariff constituted an issue during Jefferson's administration; but Jefferson and his advocates were in favour of war with England in consequence of their partiality for France, and the Federalists were in favour of peace with England in consequence of their hostility to France. The majority in the country, however, were in favour of Jefferson's Administration, and the Federalists committed harikari by holding a secret convention at Hartford, in which they were believed to have recommended the secession of the New England States, which had principally suffered from the war. Jefferson's party, therefore, was left in undisputed control of the field, and was enabled by the absence of any opposition to close its war with England without settling the only question at controversy between the two nations. The absence of any issue at the close of this war made the existence of any party unnecessary; the result of it was that all political organisations disappeared, and Monroe was elected by acclamation. This period is called in American history " the era of good feeling."

The absence of conflicting parties, however, did not prevent the period of Monroe's administration from being full of important legislation. The slavery question was temporarily disposed of by the famous Missouri Compromise, the question of protection was fully ventilated, the constitutional right to levy protective duties discussed, and the famous Monroe doctrine promulgated.

After Monroe had served two terms and was under the unwritten rule ineligible for a third term, the election of his successor practically became a personal question. Jackson had made himself conspicuous and popular by the way in which he had handled the Seminole War; Adams had long been before the country as a man of spotless integrity and personal character; Henry Clay was well known for his ability in debate and for the service he had rendered in passing the Missouri Compromise. The question of the presidency was determined solely upon the personal qualifications of these three men. After the election of Adams the present Democratic party came into existence through the animosity of Jackson to Adams and Clay, and grew out of a faction which originally was characterised by no more ambitious name than "Jackson men."

No one can read the history of the country during this period without being forced to recognise the possibility of dispensing with party government in the United States, so long as no great issue exists requiring the machinery of party organisation for its solution. The first great issue which lifted the Jackson men to the dignity of a national party arose, not in the presidential election which closed Adams's term of office and put Jackson in the White House, but later, when the attempt to enforce the tariff set the South in open and violent opposition to the North. From that time Democracy became identified with the interests of the South as opposed to the Whig party, which was identified with the interests

of the North.   This sectional conflict was not settled
until the Republican party was found courageous
enough to recognise that the real issue was the issue
of slavery and to fight it out upon the battlefield.

The conclusion to be drawn from this brief review is that, while party government is not necessary to the administration of our national affairs, it
is necessary to the pushing of any great issue such
as the abolition of slavery and the preservation of
the Union; that, in other words, parties should arise
for dealing with an emergency, and not be maintained, as in Europe, for the mere purpose of administration.

This doctrine may seem unfamiliar and heretical
to those who have accepted the comments of Mr.
Bryce upon our institutions; but it may be well in
this connection to recall the fact that while Mr.
Bryce on one page criticises our Federal Government
because there is not enough in it of party government, on another page he lays to partisanship the
whole responsibility for municipal misgovernment,
and municipal misgovernment he characterises as
the one conspicuous failure of our institutions.   It is
not unnatural that Mr. Bryce should have criticised
a system which dispenses entirely with the element
of personal leadership, so peculiarly characteristic
of England's Parliament; but there is something
a little ingenuous about the arguments which Mr.
Bryce invokes in favour of the English system.   To
him the conflict between the Prime Minister on the
one hand and the leader of the Opposition on the

17

other has a picturesque and homeric interest which he cannot willingly dissociate from political life. He does not believe that the people can be induced to take a sufficient interest in the action of the legislature to follow the events of political life unless it is put upon a stage, as it were, with the dramatic incidents of perpetual personal conflict; and this necessity for a *mise en scène* is to his mind of sufficient importance to put out of sight the evils attending this personal conflict, to which he does not seem to have ever had his eyes fully opened. These evils have been so admirably summarised by Albert Stickney,* that it is not proposed to repeat them here; but no one who has at all considered the question can fail to recognise the defects of a system which puts at the head of its departments not the men most qualified to manage these departments, but men who by their eloquence and position have secured a certain following in Parliament; which excludes men from the office for which they are peculiarly fitted, out of considerations quite foreign to the question of efficiency; which subordinates the management of the various departments of Government to questions of a majority or minority vote of confidence in the House; which calls upon men who have upon them the burden of executive office to perform also the onerous duties of the Legislature; which ignores the fact that a man who has to choose between the detail of executive work and the excite-

---

* A True Republic, by Albert Stickney.

ment of parliamentary debate cannot but sacrifice
the one to the other; which abandons measures of
national importance in favour of those which are
most calculated to strengthen and keep up party
spirit, even on occasion creating fictitious issues to
this end; and decides as to what measures should be
taken up, not because of the merits of the measures
but because of their efficiency in keeping the party
in power. That the Conservatives should have
thrown out a reform bill, as they did in 1866, not
out of opposition to this bill, but simply for the purpose of throwing the Liberal party out of power and
stepping into power themselves; that they should
have put the country to the turmoil and expense of
a new election, have secured a majority from the
country on the ground of their opposition to this
bill and then themselves have passed the very bill
which they had previously, with deliberate hypocrisy,
opposed, is a scandal due directly to a system of
party government which forgets principles in its
passion for the display of personal animosity. This
is the system which confided the Crimean war to
such a bungler as Newcastle, almost succeeded in
eliminating so necessary a man as Palmerston, and
occasioned a resignation of the ministry at the most
inopportune moment of the whole campaign; which
in the middle of another war left the country without an administration for over two months; and
which obliged the country to dispense with the serv-
ices of such a man as Peel on such a question as
the removal of the ladies of the royal bedchamber!

Illustrations of the evils of this system of government could be multiplied *ad nauseam*. It might be described as one that tends to discourage " swapping horses " on the level and compels it when fording a dangerous stream. The toleration of it can be explained only by the historic fact that the country escaped the authority of obstinate kings by refusing supplies to the king's ministers and thus forced the king to change his ministers if he wanted supplies; and that it has never undertaken to eliminate the anomalies of its Government, because those anomalies, however great their cost, continue to serve a purpose. The fact that the system exists in the first place, and that it serves to rivet popular attention on the Government in the second, seems to furnish sufficient reason not only for its maintenance in England but for its adoption in almost every other country in Europe. Indeed, Mr. Bryce is so accustomed to regard it as the best conceivable system, that in criticising our institutions he does not think it worth while to vindicate its merits. They are assumed and unconsciously adopted as furnishing the standard by which our institutions are to be judged.

In dealing, however, with municipal misgovernment he does not hesitate to attribute it mainly to the unwarrantable intrusion of national parties into purely local affairs. As has been already pointed out, these parties have the nominating machinery in their hands, and, except on rare occasions of great popular indignation, no candidate is presented to the

suffrages of the people but those selected by party
leaders. They have become national institutions,
with organisations in each State, in each county,
in each assembly district, and in each election district. Each organisation is manned by professional
politicians, most of whom are in the enjoyment or
expectation of public office. The money required
to run these parties is obtained in part by assessment of public officers and contractors, in part by
contributions from corporations and business men
wielding large interests, and in some of our larger
cities by blackmail levied on all classes of citizens,
but particularly those who violate the law. It has
been shown that these national parties are apt to divide spoils by iniquitous agreements, and to put up
candidates who will distribute patronage as ordered,
and will administer their office for the purpose of
strengthening the party rather than with a view to
the public welfare. So prejudicial is the intervention of national parties in municipal government
recognised to be, that all through the country to-day
the demand for municipal reform practically takes
the shape of a demand for the separation of municipal government from national politics. The popular demand for good administration which drove the
rascals out of office in Brooklyn in 1893, and out of
New York in 1894, has so extended that a belief in
the possibility of separating municipal government
from national politics is spreading far and wide.
The question, however, whether the separation of
municipal government from national politics can be

in fact effected is one that still remains open to grave doubt. In many cities the elections for national and State offices take place at the same time as the elections for municipal offices, and the difficulty of eliminating party considerations from such elections has been already pointed out. But even in those cities where the municipal elections are held at a different time from national and State elections there is still one serious drawback to a complete divorce of city from national politics. Our cities are integral and essential parts of our State government, and although they are now demanding, and are likely to obtain, from the State Legislatures a very much larger share of home rule than they at present enjoy, it is idle to hope that the cities can ever be governed entirely by themselves; they can never legislate except on purely local matters. In all matters which pertain to the State, the State Legislature must remain supreme. Because, therefore, the State Legislature must always continue to make general laws for the city as well as the State, every citizen who has the interest of his city at heart is as nearly concerned in the character of the State Legislature as he is in that of his board of aldermen; indeed, it may be said that he is more concerned in the Legislature than in the board, for the Legislature has, and always must have, far larger powers. Unfortunately, however, it is the State Legislature that elects the Senators to the United States Senate, and the composition therefore of the Legislature is a matter of crucial importance to the national parties. Few

men have a larger share in the legislation of the
country than the two Senators from the State of
New York. These two Senators are elected by the
Legislature, and the same Legislature which elects
these Senators makes laws for the city of New York.
How, under these circumstances, municipal government can ever be completely divorced from national
politics it seems difficult to understand ; for, while
the citizens of New York will want to eliminate national politics from the election of members of the
Legislature which is to make laws for the city, national parties will insist upon nominating candidates
for the Legislature pledged to vote for their party in
elections to the United States Senate. At times of
such popular agitation as have recently prevailed in
New York and Brooklyn the local issue becomes of
such transcendent importance that national issues
are forgotten or put into the background ; but the
moment the wave of popular indignation has passed,
permanent political machines reassert themselves,
and partisanship inevitably resumes its sway.

While, therefore, the cry for the separation of
municipal government from national politics has
served and may still serve an admirable purpose in
ridding our municipalities of the rings which have
grown up under partisan rule, it is impossible to
close our eyes to the fact that there is a radical defect in the issue, and that no permanent municipal
party or permanent municipal sentiment can be
maintained upon this principle. This question is of
such importance that it may be well to pause for a

moment in order to review the effort to separate municipal government from national politics in the city of New York.

The City Club and the Good Government clubs which have largely contributed to the overthrow of Tammany Hall in New York, were constituted mainly to propagate the doctrine that municipal government can and should be separated from national politics. They are driven, however, at every election to confront the question as to what attitude they are to take regarding candidates for the Assembly, which are annually nominated by the national parties in the districts for which these clubs are respectively formed. In every district there has been the regular Tammany nomination, Tammany claiming to be the Democratic organisation in the city. Under these circumstances, the party to which the Good Government clubs would naturally look for a good candidate is the Republican. It so happens, however, that the Republican party cannot be always counted upon for a good candidate. In 1893, in the Twenty-first Assembly District, the candidate of the Republican party was so unfit that Good Government Club A was unable to endorse him; indeed, before he was nominated, Club A informed the Republican leaders that it would be obliged to withhold its endorsement and run an independent candidate unless they consented to nominate a less objectionable man. The protest of Club A was unavailing; the result was a three-cornered fight in the district between the Tammany candidate, the

Republican candidate, and the Independent candidate of Club A; and by a division of the anti-Tammany vote, owing to the nomination of separate candidates by the Republicans and the Good Government Club, the Tammany man was elected. This case is only cited as a single illustration of the quandary in which these Good Government Clubs are likely to find themselves placed regularly every year. Nor is it the only difficulty that confronts them. When, in 1894, the same Good Government Club found itself called upon to confront the question of nominations to the Assembly and the Board of Aldermen, it secured from the Republican party the nomination of two men whom it was able to support both on the ground of personal character and on that of political conviction. It turned out, however, that most of the Democrats in the club were bitterly opposed to the nomination of two Republicans from the same district, and nothing but the overwhelming importance of the local issue prevented a large defection of Democrats from the club in consequence.

In other years, when the local issue is not so important, it is difficult to believe that these excellent clubs will not suffer largely from the effort to disregard national politics in elections to the Legislature. This difficulty can be eliminated by an amendment of the United States Constitution, by which the elections of the United States Senate will be taken out of the State Legislature and given to the people. But an amendment to the United States Constitution is so difficult a thing to bring about under any circumstances, and the opposition to this particular amendment would be so considerable, owing to many reasons upon which it is not necessary here to enlarge, that the prospect of any relief from this source must be put out of consideration for the present. Under these circumstances the question very naturally presents itself: If municipal reformers are wrong in believing that they can ever separate municipal government from national politics, and if municipal misgovernment arises from the intervention of national politics into municipal affairs, where is the remedy?

Before attempting to suggest a remedy, it is advisable to recall the fact that parties have not in America the permanence that they have in Europe; on the contrary, they come into existence upon great issues, and should of right disappear when these issues are disposed of. That they do not disappear is due to the tendency of the institution to survive the principle, as the Church tends to survive the religious idea, and the dinner-giving guilds have survived in London the charitable purpose for which they were originally constituted.

The political situation, then, which confronts us is one of singular interest: Two powerful national parties, solidly intrenched in public office, each of them controlled by a few crafty and ambitious leaders, are engaged in keeping alive fictitious issues for the sake of keeping power in themselves. The issue

between Free Trade and Protection may in itself be
a real one, but in the hands of the existing national
parties it is a fictitious one, because neither of these
parties is engaged in a sincere and dispassionate
study of the commercial problems involved, but both,
on the contrary, are pledged to a passionate and extreme view, not because such an extreme view is
best for the country, but because it is necessary to
their existence. As a matter of fact, the country
will prosper under the present Wilson Tariff bill; it
would prosper under absolute Free Trade; it would
even have prospered under the McKinley tariff; but
no country with less unlimited resources than the
United States could continue to live at all under the
desperate condition of suspense and lack of confidence which has prevailed since Mr. Cleveland's tariff reform message to Congress of December, 1887.
In other words, the country can do without Free
Trade, and Protection cannot very much injure it;
but repeated changes from one to the other jeopardise the welfare of even so resourceful a country as
ours. Not only has experience demonstrated this to
be the fact, but the most ordinary commercial common sense might have anticipated it. How is it
possible for a merchant to put in a sufficient stock
of European goods if he has reason to believe that
before he can sell these goods a change in the tariff
will involve him in incalculable loss? Or, how can
a manufacturer proceed with any sort of confidence
when a change in the tariff may at any time flood
the market with a foreign article admitted by a

lower tariff to disastrous competition with his?
And the same causes which make it impossible for
either the merchant or the manufacturer to keep his
business up to the normal demands of the country,
serve to create an unwillingness on the part of the
banker to give facilities of credit under conditions
likely to prove disastrous to those to whom credit
is given.   The result is that even those merchants
and manufacturers who, disregarding the dangers of
the situation, are willing to extend their business,
find themselves crippled by a limitation of credit
inspired by the very same want of confidence which
already serves to restrict commercial enterprise in
other directions; and as the banker will not furnish
funds to the merchant and manufacturer under such
dangerous conditions, money becomes plentiful, interest goes down, incomes diminish, and diminishing
incomes necessitate diminished expenditures. There
is no longer, therefore, a normal demand for goods,
and the anxieties of the merchant and manufacturer
are further increased by the failure to sell even the
narrow line of goods which they respectively manu-
facture or import.   And so what with the check on
business arising from fear of changes in the tariff,
and what with the check on business arising from a
diminished ability on the part of the public to buy,
we have a condition of depression which no country
less wealthy than the United States could have borne
so long.

And this regrettable condition of things is not
due to any cause which is beyond our control: it is

due to the existence of two national parties that use
the issue of Free Trade and Protection as a club
against one another, regardless of the consequences
to the nation whose interests they each with more
or less unconscious hypocrisy pretend respectively to
promote.

What the commercial community in America
needs to-day is rest, and this is what neither party is
able to give it. The blessings with which the respective parties dower us at present are commercial depression, municipal misgovernment, and a depraved
public conscience.

The fact is, our existing national parties have
fallen into the hands of a few political leaders who
have no regard for anything save their own ambition
and interest; and so long as the machinery for nominating candidates is left in their hands the citizen
can expect no permanent political improvement; all
he can do is to change one bad master for another.
It may be contended that the existing political situation in New York to-day does not maintain this
contention. The sweeping overthrow of Tammany
Hall at the recent elections seems to indicate that
good administration can be secured even under the
existing system of party government. Such a conclusion, however, is entirely without foundation.
The overthrow of Tammany Hall was a conquest
not only over a corrupt political organisation but
over both political parties. The indignation of the
people occasioned the appointment of a Committee

of Seventy, whose express object was to put up a
ticket irrespective of either party, and to which both
parties would be compelled by an overwhelming
public opinion to consent. The special task of the
Committee of Seventy was to eliminate party questions from the municipal campaign, and to find candidates of such personal worth that neither party
could presume to put up an independent ticket
against them. This the Committee of Seventy succeeded in doing, not, however, without immense
difficulty. It may seem, now that the result has
been attained, as though the task accomplished by
the Committee of Seventy has been an easy one; but
those who watched the progress of the committee
step by step know not only how difficult the task
was, but how very nearly it entirely failed of accom-
plishment, owing to the narrow spirit of partisanship which still so widely prevails. There is no
doubt but that Tammany would to-day be in power
in this city had the Committee of Seventy failed in
this task, for in that case the anti-Tammany forces
would have been divided, the Republicans would
have put up one ticket, the State Democrats another,
and the Committee of Seventy or Good Government
Club a third; and there is little doubt but that in
such a four-cornered fight Tammany would have secured a majority. The conclusion to be drawn from
recent efforts is not that good government can be
obtained under the present party system, but that it
can only be obtained when local issues are sufficiently overwhelming to temporarily set aside the

party system. Neither can it be said that the ticket put up by the Committee of Seventy was one entirely beyond criticism. The selection of some of the candidates was admittedly above reproach; that of others, on the contrary, was inspired not by considerations of fitness for office but by the necessities of placating warring factions.

It is very natural that there should prevail to-day a feeling of satisfaction that popular government had justified itself, and a consequent relapse into inactivity; but the security now enjoyed by most of our fellow-citizens as regards the future is without foundation. Evil remains organised in the halls of Tammany; the national parties are ready now as ever to divide the forces which can successfully oppose Tammany; and when the shameful disclosures of the Lexow Committee have been forgotten, the city will doubtless return to its normal servility to Tammany Hall, unless, indeed, more has been learned during the last quarter of a century than during that which preceded the previous triumph and overthrow of the same pernicious organisation. It cannot be contended that a system of government which keeps us twenty-five years at a time under the heel of such a gang of ruffians as those that gathered around Tweed of old, or around Croker in later years, and gives us only a few months of good government under the explosive action of a citizens' committee, is one which reflects credit upon popular institutions. Unless, therefore, some force can be found in the community that will substitute for

these periodic convulsions a constant watch and
check upon the administration of our affairs, there
is little chance of securing in any of our cities sta-
bility as well as efficiency of administration. Such
a force has to be developed through the evolution of
political character in a manner altogether similar to
that in which the courage of calm became evolved
out of the courage of ferocity, the peace of love out
of the fury of passion, and the justice of man out
of the injustice of Nature. The process is the same,
and the result may be the same; indeed, the process
has gone already so far that the result no longer
seems unattainable. We have already traced the
transfer of sovereignty from the crown to the people; we have seen into what impotent hands the
sovereignty then fell, and have derived courage from
the slow but sure increase in strength and wisdom
which the people have evinced. It was inevitable
that the people which had been accustomed to be
loyal to a person rather than to a principle should
remain disposed to blindly follow leaders, rather than
to laboriously work out the theories of government
for themselves and persistently adhere to them. It
was only through the disappointments that personal
leadership must bring, that the people could at last
learn that self-government means not servile obedience to a chief, but independent and consistent ad-
herence to a principle. As has already been pointed
out, it has been the good fortune of our country to
have been at certain periods in a position to dispense with party government altogether, as when

the issue of centralisation disappeared by the death
of the Federal party shortly before 1820, or as when
the issues of the war disappeared after the recon-
struction of the Southern States. In 1820 there resulted a total eclipse of national parties; at the later
period national parties did not dissolve, but there
sprang up a small though growing tendency towards
independence in politics. This independence has
given rise to what has been contemptuously termed
by partisans the mugwump.

The mugwump became recognised in politics
upon the moral issue raised by the question whether
a man against whom charges of political corruption
had been consistently made and not successfully re-
sisted should be elected to the highest office in the
land. The disaffection which defeated Blaine and
elected Cleveland was the first notice to national
parties of the survival in the country of the moral
sentiment which had lifted the abolitionists from
contempt and insignificance in the fifties to undisputed possession of the entire country in 1865. The
mugwump was overwhelmed by the craze for protection in 1888; but in 1892, after the country had
tasted the consequences of putting the Republican
party back in power, the question arose as to who
was to lead what was likely to be the triumphant
democracy, and the issue between the practical politician and the mugwump was once more raised in
the conflicting personalities of David B. Hill and
Grover Cleveland. The crushing defeat of Hill at
the Chicago convention and the nomination of

18

Cleveland was a sure indication of the strength of moral sentiment in the country; but this did not serve as any notice to the practical politician. David B. Hill pursued his devious methods as though he had not been defeated by moral sentiment at Chicago. He found a pliant tool in Isaac H. Maynard, whose tampering with official documents wrested the Senate of the State of New York from the Republican party to which it belonged and gave it to the Democrats. When Hill sought to reward Maynard by the nomination to the Court of Appeals, the mugwumps once more demonstrated their strength by defeating Maynard with an overwhelming majority. In the same election the same spirit of political independence destroyed the machine in Brooklyn, and the following election has achieved a still more signal triumph in New York.

All this goes to show that the spirit of partisanship, which Mr. Bryce thinks so essential to securing public attention to public affairs, is gradually giving way to a spirit of independence which is as pregnant with blessings for the State as was the protest of Martin Luther for the Christian Church.

How large is the number of citizens capable of independent political action in New York city can be measured by the difference between the vote for the Tammany candidate for mayor in 1892 and that for the Tammany mayor in 1894. In 1892 Thomas F. Gilroy, the Tammany candidate, received 173,510 votes, the opposing candidate, 97,923. The majority of Tammany Hall, therefore, was 75,000. In 1894 the anti-Tammany candidate, William L. Strong, received 154,094, and H. J. Grant, the Tammany candidate, 108,907. The anti-Tammany candidate, therefore, had a majority of over 45,000 votes. The difference, therefore, consists of the sum of 45,000 and 75,000, or 120,000. Out of a total vote, therefore, of about 270,000 there was a displacement of about 120,000 votes within a period of two years. This indicates the actual existence in New York of a large body of voters capable of being influenced by moral considerations, and of defeating political factions however systematically organised. When allowance is made for the fact that there is no permanent organisation of the better element, except such as has been begun by the organisation of social clubs to this end, the result of this last election cannot but give great hope to those who believe in popular institutions.

And now we are in a position to make a partial answer to the question, What is the real remedy for misgovernment, whether in our municipalities or elsewhere? The error of the belief that municipal government can only be good on condition of separation from national politics has already been pointed out. So long as the same Legislature which makes laws for the city, elects United States Senators, it is impossible to effect the separation so much to be desired. National parties must and will interfere. It is not therefore upon the narrow basis of this single issue that the disinterested element in the community must be organised for political purposes; it is rather upon the broader principle that self-government in politics differs in no essential quality from self-government in our individual lives. Both require the perpetual exercise of intelligence and self-restraint; neither is possible unless it is guided by that order of sentiment which has been heretofore defined as religious.

To expect that religion, even in the large sense in which this word is used in these pages, can within any reasonable time consciously exert an influence in our politics, would be as unreasonable as to expect any single effort of a single mind or pen to induce sensual men to give up the satisfaction of their senses, or to enable irascible men for ever after to control their temper. All that has been attempted here is to give additional reason to those whose lives are more or less influenced by the religious sentiment for extending to the political field the moral efforts which have, till to-day, been so generally confined to individual conduct. Partisanship is as essential a factor in political life as hunger, thirst, aversion, to pain, and sexual desire are necessary factors in the private lives of every one of us. It cannot be disregarded; it cannot be destroyed; it must be recognised and handled. The larger the number of persons in the community, whether men or women, who have a clear apprehension and appreciation of this, the larger the hope that this great experiment of popular government which our country is now making will succeed, and will not, by failure, put humanity back to where it was before the middle ages. It is not enough, however, to say that the problem of partisanship must be dealt with; the matter of essential importance to us is, How?

It would be unwise, if not impossible, to lay down any programme for disposing of this difficulty, which, because it takes its roots in defects of human temperament, must always be more or less with us. As a matter of fact, it is now being dealt with by the organisation of manifold groups brought together with some common purpose, as, for example, for the purpose of securing civil service reform, excise reform, municipal reform, educational reform, all of which have a general tendency to keep watch over the action of national parties in the administration of our affairs. There is hardly a large town in the country which has not to-day some form of society engaged in the task of endeavouring to secure good municipal government. In the city of New York there are now actually at work to this end the City Club, the Good Government clubs, the City Vigilance League, and the Committee of Seventy. These four organisations tend to overlap and sometimes to conflict with one another; they will doubtless be driven eventually to find some form of co-operation; circumstances will force upon them the conviction that good government can never be permanently secured until the machinery for nominating candidates is taken out of the hands in which it now is; or until there exists some association powerful enough either to hold primaries of its own or to make an organised effort to control the primaries of the national parties. When they have effected this they will be exposed to a new danger —that is to say, capture by ambitious or interested men who will utilize their activity for personal ends. So long as ambition and temper are the main factors in bringing about movements towards good government it cannot be expected that they will long remain true to their original principles. There must be a higher motive at the helm—the motive that prompts men to self-improvement in domestic life. The conflict with evil in the political arena is no other in kind than the conflict with evil which every religious man is more or less waging in his own heart. We are led by these considerations to the final question, What direct part, if any, can religion play in the political field? The discussion of this matter we postpone to the final chapter.

CHAPTER XIV.

BEFORE attempting to draw a conclusion from the various considerations contained in the foregoing chapters it will be a convenience briefly to sum up those to which we have already arrived, in an order somewhat different, but for our present purpose more direct, than that employed in the context.

The history of Evolution divides itself into two epochs: The first, in which the principle of natural selection had its own way unchecked in the world; the second, throughout which the principle of natural selection has been in a great measure defeated by the more or less conscious efforts of man.

During the first epoch the principle of the survival of the fittest put man at the head of the predatory system. This system tended to divide animals into those who hunted and those who were hunted. The former tended automatically to improve their weapons of attack; the latter continued automatically to improve their weapons of defence or flight. Ferocity was the quality developed in the

269

one, and fear that developed in the other. But the ferocity that served to put the great carnivora at the head of the predatory system served also to render individuals of the same species unfit for social life. The great carnivora, therefore, are solitary animals. On the other hand, the intelligence which enabled man by the use of tools to make himself more dreaded than the strongest of the carnivora made it also possible for man to accommodate himself to social life. The exactions of social life put upon him the necessity of self-restraint, and through self-restraint gradually developed qualities that tended to differentiate him from other animals more characteristically than any mere increase in cerebral development. In other words, man became different from the lower animals more by virtue of his moral than by virtue of his intellectual qualities. Gradually the pleasure that attends the exercise of any self-improving faculty converted the arduous exercise of self-restraint under the compulsion of fear, into a willing exercise of self-restraint under the stimulus of love of approbation. Meanwhile there gradually developed in man's mind a faculty of attaining abstract ideas, and out of that faculty sprang speculation regarding his origin and mission. These and other kindred questions have been defined as religious. Religion created a new set of motives which, acting in co-operation with the exactions of social life, gradually converted the qualities which man derived from his savage ancestors into virtues which are characteristically opposed to those from which they are derived. Thus passion became converted into love, which has been shown to be so different from passion as almost to exclude it. Fear became converted into reverence, ferocity into courage; reverence being respect without fear, and courage nerve without ferocity. A study of the development of passion and ferocity into love and courage demonstrates the large part which human effort has played in the transformation. Now this human effort has been directed against the animal instincts—that is to say, against those qualities which, through the process of Evolution, had put man at the head of the predatory system. One of the tendencies, therefore, of man's effort has been to diminish his ability to hold his own in the struggle for existence; for love in the advance of civilisation tends to degenerate, through luxury, into lasciviousness, and courage to disappear with the disuse of ferocity.

But man did not confine his efforts against Nature to moral qualities alone. As his knowledge of Nature increased he became more and more able to distinguish between those forces of Nature which contributed to his advancement and those which threatened his survival. He learned how to utilise the very forces of Nature which tended to destroy him, and has succeeded in violating some of the fundamental principles of Evolution without as yet exhibiting any fatal symptom of degeneration. On the contrary, not only does he still maintain his place at the head of the animal kingdom, carnivorous and other, but his supremacy seems to be more and more finally and absolutely determined. To-day man's whole existence is a tribute to what human effort can do in its battle with Nature. This battle is admirably compared by Prof. Huxley to the struggle of man with adverse conditions in the familiar process of horticulture.* The essential fact to be kept in mind in studying the progress of man in relation to the principles of Evolution is that the principles of Evolution, as observable in the development of the lower animals, can in no way be applied to the development of man; for man is capable of counteracting Nature in two ways: First, by his intelligence, and, second, by his faculty of choice.

By his intelligence he utilises the very forces which prove deadly to the lower animals. By his faculty of choice, or by his faculty for creating the greater inclination, he is able, by efforts of his own, to encourage in himself the development of motives diametrically opposed to those which are the product of the struggle for existence; and if we are to believe the testimony of our consciousness, he is developing a faculty which can deliberately refuse to follow the more attractive inclination in order to obey the dictates of a sentiment, obedience to which is attended by disappointment, without any prospect of thereby avoiding future pain or enjoying future pleasure.

---

* Huxley's Essays, Prolegomena to Evolution and Ethics.

Whether this so-called faculty of choice exists is questioned by those who regard man as the slave of the greater inclination. This theory would make the Creator himself the slave of his greater inclination, and proceeds upon the assumption that every effect is caused. In assuming that every effect must be caused, it fails to take into account the fact that we have no explanation to give for the creation of force or matter, for the creation of life, for the creation of consciousness, and that these great appearances were, so far as we know, uncaused.

If the faculty of consciousness came into the world uncaused, why not the faculty of choice?

But even if it be impossible to maintain the existence of a faculty of choice in man, it cannot be disputed that man has a faculty by effort of his own to contribute to the making of his greater inclination. If, then, he can make his greater inclination, he is the master of that very determining factor of which the determinists endeavour to make him the slave. To say of man that he is the slave of an inclination of which he is master, is to juggle with words. If man is master of his greater inclination, he can, by his own efforts, gradually so develop the religious inclination as to make it continuously superior to the animal. When he attains this he has attained perfection.

The word religious just used requires explanation. Religions have differed not only in their origin but in their nature. It is difficult to find anything in common between the Greek and the Hebrew religion. The Greek religion seems to spring from ancestral pride and to be unconcerned with ethics. In the Hebrew religion, on the contrary, there is no trace of ancestral pride, and it is essentially a code of ethics.

The Greek religion, if it is to be compared at all to that of Israel, India, or China, must be made to include philosophy, from which, however, it was characteristically distinguished.

Religion in these later years is mainly occupied with two things : First, theology—that is to say, speculation as regards matters not included in the domain of science ; and, second, ethics—that is to say, the determination of rules of conduct. Theology tends to be confounded with philosophy and ethics with law. In both theology and ethics, the dominant problem is that of pain. In theology an effort is made to square the existence of pain with justice. In ethics an effort is made, by laying down rules of conduct to be obeyed by all, to diminish the total of pain to be endured by all. Science has demonstrated that in the process of Evolution pleasure gradually tends to attend the exercise of faculties which conduce to perpetuating the life of the individual and of the race, whereas pain attends acts which conduce to the destruction of the individual or race. Science also teaches that an evolution of conduct has attended the evolution of function, and that an extension of sympathy has attended both. The conclusion has been drawn from this fact that the processes of Evolution are sufficient in themselves to complete the evolution of conduct and the extension of sympathy so as to bring man to a state of perfection. But this theory neglects to take into account many important facts. In the first place, the principle of natural selection and the survival of the fittest through which Evolution took place in its first epoch have in great part ceased. The conclusions, therefore, that have been drawn from operations in the past cannot be made to apply without great discrimination to the future. In the second place, man is no longer conforming himself to the principles of Evolution; he is fighting them. Hence can be drawn the same conclusion as before. In the third place, owing to this conflict between man and Nature, pleasure and pain are no longer guides to conduct. On the contrary, man has now to endure pain and to forego pleasure, sometimes in order to escape a greater future pain or enjoy a greater future pleasure, sometimes in obedience to what has been called religious sentiment, because it is in opposition to the instinct of the lower nature.

The special characteristic of the second epoch of Evolution is that in it man plays an independent rôle; he is no longer being automatically developed by blind processes of Evolution, but is himself directing the forces of Evolution, and sometimes opposing them.

In so far as man is consciously and by the exercise of effort overcoming brutal instincts and replacing them by spiritual virtues he is approaching perfection, not through the process of evolution but in spite of it. How far man will proceed on the road to perfection depends chiefly upon himself.

It is impossible to estimate how large a part religion has played in making man able and willing to exercise the effort indispensable to progress on the road to perfection. This is due to the fact that different men are differently constituted, one man being almost without religious sentiment, and therefore little, if at all, subject to religious impulse. Such a man may nevertheless be guided by intelligent apprehension of his duty to his neighbour, which will guide his conduct so that it will hardly be distinguishable from that of a religious life. Another man, on the contrary, is so constituted that, although deficient in intelligence and sense of duty, he is keenly alive to religious sentiment and religious impulse, and is by this religious impulse rendered capable of the self-restraint which is essential to peace and prosperity in social life. These two types of men will necessarily estimate the part played by religion in the progress of man in an entirely opposite manner. The recognition, however, of the fact that these two types of men exist makes it impossible for the irreligious man not to admit that so long as the religious type exists religion has an essential rôle to play in the world.

Religion must not be confounded with the institutions that have grown up out of it. Religion fighting Christian civilisation with the sword of

Mahomet was a scourge; religion fighting the advancement of knowledge with a papal bull was equally a scourge; but neither of these attacks upon the progress of man is to be attributed to religion; both are to be attributed to the human institutions which grew up in the name of religion and in spite of it. The superstitions that survive to-day must not be put to the account of religion, but to the account of human imperfection, from which religion always has suffered and must always suffer. But while it is essential to the progress of man that religion, in the sense of the word in which it has been used in these pages, should continue to be the dominant influence in determining human conduct, it must also be recognised that the Church, in which religion has made its sanctuary—whether the Church be Roman or Greek, Catholic or Protestant, Jew or Gentile—has acquired a control over the hearts of men which is too intimately associated with the religious influence itself to be lightly set aside. To a large part of civilised humanity the Church *is* religion; and so long as this is the case the Church must not only be tolerated, but respected and maintained even by those who denounce its superstitions and deplore its error. There has grown, however, and is growing daily, a conviction that the Church is not doing the work which it should do in the world; and nowhere is the failure to do its work more conspicuous than in those countries where monarchical or aristocratic institutions have given way to popular government. The inherent evils of party gov-

ernment in England and France, and the total depravity of municipal administration in America, all
tend to discredit popular government. The neutral
attitude of the Church in England and America, and
its positive hostility to the republican form of government in France, have given rise to loud denunciation, and the Church has been called upon by
some to assert control over the public as well as the
private lives of its parishioners. But the history of
Church and State clearly indicates the unwisdom of
such a course.

Again, a careful study of Christian ethics brings
out forcibly the fact that they have got out of touch
with the needs of humanity in more than one particular. Christianity aims at perfection, whereas a
code of ethics which does not recognise the weakness of humanity is incapable of determining its
conduct. Moreover, Christ was an ascetic ; he taught
not only disregard of the body but its mortification.
Asceticism is now repudiated by the sincerest religious
thought of the day, and a due regard for the body
is recognised as essential to a wholesome spiritual
life. Last, but not least, Christ preached to the inhabitants of a conquered province. Obedience was
the cardinal virtue of public life not only at the
time of Christ but for fifteen centuries after him.
The gospels, therefore, both in their aims at perfection, in their teaching of asceticism, and in the absence
of instruction as regards the relation of man to the
State under a form of government in which his public duty to the State is as important as his private

duties to his family, are, it must be admitted, incomplete and inadequate. As a matter of fact, that part of Christ's teaching which is impracticable to-day has been silently dropped, or been, by a pious fraud, treated as allegory. Thus modified it still remains the greatest spiritual message that has ever come to the world. As a guide, therefore, to individual conduct it is a potent factor for good; as a guide to public conduct it is entirely without force or effect.

And it has been shown that the Church had best keep strictly away from all intervention in matters of State. From every point of view, therefore, it does not seem as though the Church, *quâ* Church, could directly attack the political difficulties with which civilisation is now confronted.

An examination of the political difficulties just referred to brings out the undoubted fact that practically every great problem which now faces humanity is a political one. The problems of pauperism and socialism, of education and crime, can only be handled by the State. Pity, acting through the instrumentality of the Church, cannot be prevented from invading the province of the State in all these matters, but it is an invasion which, if unintelligently indulged in, tends to debilitate the Church, to serve as an excuse for inefficacy on the part of the State, and to keep alive the very difficulties it seeks to suppress. The State, owing to the failure of religious men to discern the religious character of their polit-

19

ical duties, has fallen into the hands of professional politicians, who do not pretend, in America, to be actuated by any but mercenary motives, and who, even in England and France, would smile at the thought of introducing the ethics of Christianity into the workings of their Foreign Office. Ambition is the best motive that animates politicians in all three countries; but the motive which prevails in America is undoubtedly the desire for political plunder, and the invasion of politics by this spirit in France and England cannot long be postponed.

This is the situation that concerns us. What, if any, is the remedy?

It is with reluctance that a remedy for so profound an evil is suggested. Especially is this the case in view of the fact that no single panacea for such evils as infest politics can be propounded. But many such panaceas in which religion and science are more or less involved have been proposed, some of them containing elements of utility that should not be neglected, some of them containing also suggestions that indicate confusion as regards the relation of religion and science to one another and to the State. These relations have been considered at some length, because it is believed that if they are properly understood the remedies proposed would possibly be modified. If the conclusions which have been arrived at are sound, it is clear that the Church, as such, cannot undertake the work for which, in many respects, it seems so admirably fitted.

But though the Church may not be an instrument through which the work can be effected, it seems clear, beyond the possibility of refutation, that it is through religion only that the work of regeneration can effectually be accomplished. And it is because in this statement so much depends upon the meaning attributed to the word religion that just what religion is has carefully been studied and as nearly as possible defined. That the religious spirit has been conspicuous by its absence in modern politics is beyond dispute. That its interference in matters political was by no means an unmixed good in the middle ages would hardly to-day be questioned; and yet, that it is the only motive which can make self-government possible, seems the necessary conclusion to be drawn from the failure of popular institutions when left to ambition and self-interest as contrasted with the general advance in popular morality under the stimulus of an intelligent effort at self-restraint. In other words, what the Church in its errors and abuses is to religion, the political machine is to true political principles. The religious spirit—remembering always that by religious spirit is meant the desire and resolution to fight animal instinct in so far as it clashes against spiritual instincts essential to social life—pervades the people. It has built up the Church and tends to correct the encroachment of the machine; but the struggle between the religious spirit and natural instinct is a perpetual one, and in politics at the present day there is no doubt but that the machine, except in isolated places and under exceptional circumstances, is supreme. It has been pointed out, however, that the supremacy of the machine is due to the abdication of the people, and that this again is the natural consequence of a change from monarchical to democratic institutions. The sceptre passed from the king to the people, but the people remained uninstructed as to the duties of the government which they assumed. The Church failed in its duty to instruct them because the Church was itself averse to the change, and because there was nothing in the ethics of the Church that concerned the public duties of the citizen. And so religious people, both within the pale of the Church and without it, have learned to regard politics as a matter of concern to politicians only and not as a matter of responsibility for themselves. So reconciled have they become to this theory that many of them have given up the effort at securing good government altogether, and entertain and preach the doctrine that more can be done by co-operating with spoilsmen than by opposing them. The problem presented by crime and pauperism has been carefully studied with a view to pointing out how utterly present methods fail to deal with it, and how much of the failure is due to the political machines to which the handling of this problem has been intrusted. The religious spirit, working through private channels, has not been found to be able either to check or to co-operate usefully with municipal authorities selected upon the principle of spoils. Nothing but an overturn of the spoils sys-

tem itself, and the selection of good municipal officers, liberated by a sound civil service system from
the tyranny of partisanship, offers any chance of an
intelligent solution of this great problem.

Again, earnest people have not awakened to the
importance of educating their partners in the difficult work of government. The mistake of confiding
this task to a press which, exposed as it is to commercial competition, perpetually tends to descend to
the level of that newspaper which appeals most successfully to the lowest tastes in the community, has
been pointed out. Education upon a commercial
basis has never succeeded. All our recognised educational institutions are heavily endowed, and are to
that extent, therefore, eleemosynary in their character. The greatest educational work of all is that
of the press, because it operates on a man during by
far the longest part of his life, and because the
lessons it teaches are drawn from the events which
immediately surround him, and are immediately
translated into action, through which the whole
country must either suffer or succeed. Appeal must
be made to the spirit which founds hospitals, universities, and asylums, to endow an organ which can
afford to state facts as they are, free from financial,
commercial, or partisan bias.

Again, the tremendous power of the workingman,
gradually informing himself and awakening to his
strength, can no longer be overlooked by those who
desire to see our present civilisation maintained.
This power, if educated, can be ranged on the side

of order, whereas if allowed to run riot it is likely, in its war upon capital, to destroy the very foundations upon which our civilisation is built.

All these considerations, taken in connection with the gospel of effort which has been preached since the days of Buddha, but which the doctrines of determinism and *laissez faire*, drawing false deductions from the principles of Evolution in the past, have done so much to depreciate, point to the inevitable conclusion that the time has come for earnest men to recognize that they can no longer allow politics to take care of themselves.

But it has been already pointed out that the Church *quâ* Church cannot interfere in matters of State. What, then, is the alternative?

What the Churches cannot do churchmen can do; and in this one matter they can co-operate with others as earnest as they, who are prevented by differences of creed from communion with them within the limits of their special beliefs. In other words, the study of social and political problems and the effort to solve them, is a work in which all earnest men can join irrespective of those differences of creed which now separate them. Indeed, there is in the present condition of things an opportunity for compensation of no ordinary kind. Those men who are fitted by the disinterestedness of their motives, by intelligence and education, to grapple with the problems of the day, have heretofore been excluded from the advantages of co-operation as churchmen by differences of creed, and as politicians by differences of partisanship. They have been kept asunder by barriers which are to a large extent imaginary; for although the differences of temperament which characterise the Methodist and the Roman Catholic are likely eternally to keep them apart in matters of creed and theology, there is, as a matter of fact, no reason which should prevent their co-operation in the effort to solve the problems of pauperism, of socialism, and of self-government; and although the differences of interest and education that separate free traders from protectionists are not likely to disappear, there is no fundamental reason why Republicans and Democrats should not join in the same effort. The preceding chapters have been written for the purpose of demonstrating the necessity and possibility of such co-operation; all that remains now to suggest is the practical steps by which this co-operation can be effected.

And, in the first place, what can the Church do in this direction? If the clergy were persuaded that the duty of a citizen to study social problems and organise for the purpose of solving them was as paramount as that of charity and unselfishness, it is difficult to conceive how priests and ministers could fail to urge this duty upon their parishioners. Nor should their words consist of vague exhortations to public spirit. The clergy do not confine themselves to vague exhortations when the life of some charity or mission is at stake. They organise societies, they raise subscriptions, they appoint times and places for meetings, they select committees, and they take all the steps that are necessary to put the machinery in operation necessary to obtain tangible results. An effort has been made in these pages to demonstrate that the most powerful engine for grappling with the problem of pauperism is the city department that deals with the subject of charity and correction. If this be true, the spirit and enthusiasm which has heretofore been employed in organising private charities should now be employed in organising effort to achieve more fruitful results through the more powerful operation of public office.

The first objection that will be made to this suggestion is that the clergy cannot interfere in politics. This argument proceeds upon a profound misconception of the facts. It is not because political machines have chosen to invade, capture, and corrupt the administration of our municipal affairs that, for that reason, city administration must necessarily be admitted to form a part of politics, in the sense in which this word is generally used. Politics have their limitations as well as religion. It is as great an outrage on our liberties for the Democratic party in the State of New York, for its own advantage, to seize upon the remunerative offices of our Department of Charities and Correction, as it would be for the Roman Catholic Church to do so. The real confusion in the matter consists in the fact that people generally confound politics with partisanship. This is what a clergyman does when he refuses to

interest himself in public charity because of its supposed political complexion. Nevertheless, it must
be admitted that, as a matter of fact, the administration of our public charities is political in the largest
and truest sense of the word; so is the question of
public education; so is the question of the press; so
is the question of an incorruptible police, of gambling, of prostitution. Is it conceivable that the
clergy will maintain that they have a right to exhort
their congregation as to the iniquity of indecency at
home, but must remain silent when that indecency
stalks unblushing through the streets?—that they
have a right to instruct on the question of education
when the parishioner is wealthy enough to educate
his children by private tuition, but must remain
silent however great the abuse in the public instruction of that vast majority of children who must look
for their education to the State? Is it conceivable
that the clergy, once persuaded that our present system of dealing with the pauper is one that manufac-
tures paupers faster than any private charity can
relieve, will continue to consume its own energy and
the energy of its parishioners in keeping alive the
very evil which it is its intention to suppress? It
would be impossible to find a better illustration of
the evil effect of the incorrect use of words upon
the minds and actions of men than is contained in
the misuse of this word politics. The true definition of the word is that it is the science or art of
government; that it is that part of ethics which
consists in the knowledge or practice of conducting

the various forces of a State or nation; but because
the administration of the affairs of a State or nation
has fallen into the hands of parties, the word politics
has incidentally got to include also the contests of
parties for power. These contests have in all time
developed so much that is bad and treacherous in
human nature, that the word politics has at last
become discredited, and the great battle which has
been fought between the Church and State in Europe has filled Americans with a very justifiable
horror of anything like interference on the part of
the clergy with matters political. And so there is in
this question how far, if at all, the clergy may with
propriety interest themselves in public affairs, a confusion between three very distinct ideas and prejudices. In the first place, because the administration
of the affairs of a State is essentially political in the
truest sense of the word, any interest in municipal
matters cannot be conscientiously called by any other
name than politics; but, in the second place, politics
has become confounded with partisanship, or the
struggle of parties for power; and, in the third place,
the idea of the Church becoming involved in any
such struggle for political power is rightly abhorrent
to the American mind. If, however, the real meaning of the word politics be kept carefully separate
from its derived meaning, it will be readily seen that
whereas it is a crime for the Church to become involved in the one, it is also a crime for the Church
to abstain from interest in the other.

But even this statement must be made with an

important exception, for much will depend upon
the kind of interest that the clergy take in the matter. For the clergy itself to undertake sectarian organisation with a view to political action would be
unwise and impracticable. However great the municipal evil be, if every Presbyterian church in the
city were to undertake to convert its Presbyterian
parishes into political organisations, so that the movement could be understood or misunderstood to be a
Presbyterian movement, it would tend to crystallise
against it other sects which would very justly depre-
cate the political power which any one sect could
obtain by such political action.

The Church, then, must abstain from anything
that can involve it in a struggle for political power,
and must refrain from any organisation which could
put on a semblance of sectarianism; but it is a duty
imposed upon the Church by the new condition of
things which obtained when government passed from
the hands of a class into those of the people, boldly
to preach the public duties which have thereby been
assumed; and not only to preach but to see that those
steps are taken which will lead to organised study
and fruitful action. These three conclusions serve
to indicate pretty clearly just what is the scope and
what are the limits of action permitted to the Church.
In the first place, the area or unit of organisation
must not be the parish but the political district. In
the second place, the organisation must not be sectarian, but must result from the preaching of political
action in churches of every denomination in the dis-

trict. In the third place, it must be strictly non-partisan. The first two of these conclusions suggest that the proper means of organisation would be somewhat as follows : Assuming that in one political district the wisdom of organising for the improvement of the condition of the people should make itself manifest to any one clergyman therein, he should proceed in exactly the same manner as if he desired to interest his congregation in a new charity or mission. He would consult a few of the most intelligent and influential of his parishioners. If they responded to his suggestion, the laymen selected by them would begin an organisation within the district. Before the organisation was completed communication would be opened with every other parish church in the district. An effort would be made to secure the co-operation of all the clergy therein, with the purpose of securing through the clergy that of the leading vestrymen, elders, deacons, etc., connected with the respective churches. When a name for the organisation had been found and its purposes defined, the prosperity of the association could be assured by the efforts of the clergy, even though it should be deemed best that the clergy itself be excluded from membership in its governing board. And as has been already intimated, the clergy can do more than vainly denounce and appeal. The clergy can collect subscriptions, can furnish places of meeting, and last, but not least, can set apart an hour every Sunday for the transaction of political business.

The success of every such organisation would depend upon the skill and zeal of those interested in it, but it would also depend largely upon a few questions of detail which must not be overlooked; and there probably is no matter of detail more important than what may seem at first sight a trivial question—whether an hour on Sunday should or should not be devoted to this work. There are those who would object to the use of Sunday for political purposes. No attempt will be made in these pages to convert those Sabbatarians who insist upon maintaining the Jewish theory of the day in opposition to the express teaching of Christ; but to those who are willing to listen to him who said that the Son of Man is Lord also of the Sabbath, all that seems needful in order to justify this course is to recall the fact that the work of such an association would be no less religious or fruitful than that of the priest who sanctifies the Sabbath by officiating thereon. And the very fact that the work was done on a Sunday would contribute to keep alive in such associations the religious note, without which they are likely to go the way of all other political bodies. Again, one of the principal difficulties attending the organisation of such a body as the one suggested is lack of time. The men best fitted for this task are already overworked during the week. To ask them to set aside another week-day hour for a new effort to improve municipal conditions would be asking them sometimes to do a thing which was materially impossible. If, however, Sunday evening were devoted to this work, and the usual Sunday service were abandoned for the express purpose of enabling the congregation to attend to its political duties, two objects would be accomplished. In the first place, an hour would be found which might otherwise be wanting; in the second place, it would be brought home to the congregation that the clergy was in earnest in advocating the cause, and considered the cause sufficiently imperative to advise the sacrifice of a service thereto.

As regards the general purposes of such an association there are but few suggestions that remain to be made. The preceding chapters have shown clearly enough what is the work to which it is the duty of a citizen to attend. The only point left to which attention need now be directed is as to the principal political object of such an association.

It has been already sufficiently pointed out in preceding chapters that municipal misgovernment is due to the invasion of partisanship. It has also been pointed out that the clergy can have nothing to do with any movement for improving the condition of the people unless such a movement be free from partisanship. For these two reasons, therefore, it is essential that any such association should recognise the necessity of divorcing purely municipal administration from national politics; and inasmuch as it is impossible to secure good government from rascally officials, the great purpose of such an association ought to be to see to the nomination, elec-

tion, and appointment of city officials on the ground
of fitness alone and without regard for partisanship. Such a platform would inevitably carry in its
wake an extension of the Civil Service rules, to the
importance of which our fellow-citizens do not seem
to be as yet sufficiently alive; a larger measure of
home rule for cities; separation of municipal from
national elections; a revision of our criminal law
that would permit of an indeterminate sentence; a
radical change in our treatment of the criminal
and pauper which would restore him to society
only when he had proved himself fit for it, and
make him as nearly as possible self-supporting during his reformation; a study of the questions raised
by socialism in co-operation with the workingman
and not in opposition to him; an organisation of
charity that would leave behind a spirit of gratitude
rather than one of distrust; that would seek to find
employment for the workman rather than to give
him alms; that would defend him in court, and
teach him to resist political abuses to which he has
of late shown himself so willing to succumb.

Such an association once organised successfully
in one district would gradually spring up in adjoin-
ing districts, until at last, by a confederation of these
associations, a body would be formed of formidable
strength, capable of almost any practicable achievement. Such a confederation could at no late date
endow a weekly paper which would handle public
questions in the spirit of the university rather than
in that of the partisan, and could at any rate fur-

nish facts to the public unbiased by financial need
or political considerations. It will doubtless be
found that in every place where such an organisation is needed there already exist some societies or
clubs constituted for the same purpose. This is
notably the case in the city of New York. The
plain duty of religious men would in such case be,
not to organise something new, but to enter into
the organisations already in existence, and by introducing among them the principles of concord and
forbearance, so conspicuous by their absence in most
political combinations, contribute to perseverance,
permanence, and success. The impulsive and sometimes discordant action of many associations it
would be the rôle of churchmen of all creeds and
denominations to combine into a confederation to
which every separate body would lend its strength
without losing its individuality.

It would be idle to indulge in the hope that any
such organisation could permanently dispose of the
problem of misgovernment. The very power which
such an organisation, if successful, would obtain
could not fail eventually to corrupt it; but the
argument of the spirit that doubts, which would
advise against all organisation because every organisation must eventually die either through inactivity
or corruption, is one which is equally applicable to
every effort. We make effort to live, yet we must
all eventually die. We make effort to be virtuous,
and yet few can expect to attain perfection. It is
extremely probable that such an organisation would

ultimately fall into the hands of the very enemy
against whom it is directed, but to say that for that
reason we should abstain from organisation is as
illogical as to advise against building fortifications
lest the fortifications be captured, or against putting weapons in the hands of our soldiers lest those
weapons be wrested from their hands. If such an organisation came into existence and acquired strength,
it would do good while it was strong and while it
remained steadfast to its purpose; and when, in
subsequent years, it became either inactive or corrupt, it would be the duty of future generations to
solve the new problem then presented to them.

It has been the aim of these pages to deal with
the evils that concern us in this life, and not with
those that may hereafter concern us in some other
state of existence; to deal with the present rather
than with the future, the actual rather than the possible. There is one terrible fact in existence with
which we all must reckon: this fact is pain. So far
as we can see, it is unevenly and unjustly distributed.
To some there seem to have been given all the good
things in this world, and if any shadow falls over
their lives it is mainly the shadow of themselves.
To others, on the contrary, all the good things in
this world have been denied; they have been deprived of those qualities that make them objects of
love or even pity; they are set by hideous instincts
upon injuring rather than benefiting their fellow-
creatures; they make the lives of all about them
20

wretched, until, after having inflicted untold unhappiness upon those about them, they gravitate to
the workhouse or to the penitentiary. Others, while
free from those aggressive qualities which make
them hateful to their fellow-creatures, are without
the moral or mental qualities necessary to enable
them to make their way in the world. These, because they excite our sympathy, very often create
the more unhappiness. Death, disease, and insanity
do havoc enough amongst those we hold most dear
in the world, to set some of us upon the conquest of
that large part of the kingdom of pain from which
by effort and intelligence our fellow-creatures can
still be rescued. This book will have accomplished
its purpose if it persuades a single reader that pain
can be diminished by the exercise of these faculties;
that no human being is so circumstanced but that
he can contribute to make life less hard for those
about him; that it is to religious sentiment, and to
religious sentiment alone, whether within the pale
of the Church or without, that humanity can look
for the exercise of the self-restraint necessary to this
end; that human suffering can be dealt with most
efficaciously by the action of the State; that the
commonwealth can by religious sentiment be lifted
out of the mire, where it now is, into an atmos-
phere instinct with courage and hope; that it can
become an altar to which every aspiration may turn,
before which every creed may worship, and from
which every blessing may flow, so that the humblest
worker may ultimately feel that in devoting himself

to the gospel of effort, whether in private life or in the field of politics, he is developing within himself that Godhead which centuries ago uttered those words of promise and consolation : " Come unto me, all ye that labour and are heavy laden, and I will give you rest."

THE END.

www.ingramcontent.com/pod-product-compliance
Lightning Source LLC
Chambersburg PA
CBHW031404270326

41929CB00010BA/1313